Housing and Social Exclusion

of related interest

Social Care and Housing
Edited by Ian Shaw, Susan Lambert and David Clapham
ISBN 978 1 85302 437 5
Research Highlights in Social Work 32

Children's Homes Revisited
David Berridge and Isabelle Brodie
ISBN 978 1 85302 565 5

Young People Leaving Care
Life After the children Act 1989
Bob Broad
ISBN 978 1 85302 412 2

Social Exclusion in European Cities
Processes, Experiences and Responses
Edited by Ali Madanipour, Göran Cars and Judith Allen
ISBN 978 1 85302 609 6
Regional Policy and Development 23

Housing Options for Disabled People
Edited by Ruth Bull
ISBN 978 1 85302 454 2

Housing and Social Exclusion

Edited by Fiona Spiers

Jessica Kingsley Publishers
London and Philadelphia

First published in the United Kingdom in 1999
by Jessica Kingsley Publishers
116 Pentonville Road
London N1 9JB, UK
and
400 Market Street, Suite 400
Philadelphia, PA 19106, USA

www.jkp.com

Copyright © Jessica Kingsley Publishers 1999
Printed digitally since 2010

Library of Congress Cataloging in Publication Data
A CIP catalogue record for this book is available from the Library of Congress

British Library Cataloguing in Publication Data
Housing and social exclusion
1. Mentally handicapped - Housing - Great Britain
2. Housing policy - Great Britain
I. Spiers, Fiona E.
363.5'974'0941

ISBN 978 1 85302 638 6

Contents

List of Tables

List of Figures

Acknowledgements

Festschrifts are more usually dedicated to distinguished individuals than to organisations. The decision to publish this book is a testimony to the character and success of St Anne's Shelter & Housing Action. The chapters cover the range of St Anne's work and services. The editor and all the contributors are very grateful for the interest, support and constructive comments of colleagues, whose observations and insights spark and refine new trains of thought. St Anne's appreciated the generosity of The Halifax plc for sponsoring the 'Housing 2000' Conference, where some of these papers were originally presented. Personally, I would like to thank Bill Kilgallon, Chris Clair, Tony Ryan, Gordon Costello and Ian Sissling for agreeing to share their reminisences of events at St Anne's for the years for which no records exist. Throughout the process, Bill Kilgallon OBE, Chief Executive of St Anne's, has been a source of support and encouragement, even when he disagreed with the editor's conclusions! The patience and eagle-eyed proof-reading of my colleague Laura Blinston have greatly enhanced the book's accuracy. My family, Edward, Robert and Amanda, have patiently tolerated yet another time-consuming enterprise. Finally, the contents of these essays represent the opinions of the individual contributors and should not be construed as portraying the views of St Anne's Shelter & Housing Action.

Introduction
Social Exclusion, Housing
and Community Care

The belief that everyone is entitled to the chance of decent housing and the right to a full life in the community has dominated the evolution of St Anne's Shelter & Housing Action. From its very foundation, the organisation has sought to access accommodation for those in housing need, then help them resettle in that accommodation and stabilise their lifestyle. As the organisation developed from services for homeless people and for those with alcohol problems into a major provider of care in the community for people with mental health problems and learning disabilities, the access to and provision of good quality, appropriate housing was at the heart of St Anne's vision and growth. In addition to its residential provision, St Anne's has developed a significant amount of move-on accommodation where formerly homeless people can lead an independent life with as much or as little support as they need, and a variety of resettlement schemes to help homeless people across the bridge from social exclusion into housing.

Contributions to the volume have been invited to illustrate both a service provider's perspective on recent developments on housing the socially excluded and the impact of national developments on a local service provider in the mixed economy of social care, and to suggest future trends in housing and community care. This book focuses on the community care provided by one local voluntary organisation, in the hope that it will be of interest to those who work in similar organisations in the front-line as well as to commentators and students. St Anne's sets out to provide its range of services extremely well, to be models of good practice and frequently also of innovation; it does not claim to be able to cater for every group covered by the blanket provisions of Care in the Community.

For nearly forty years, community care has been hailed as desirable. The very name suggests that vulnerable people receive the interest and concern they need in a supportive environment. Its impact was first felt by people with mental health problems in the 1960s as the advent of new anti-psychotic drugs enabled an emphasis on treatment rather than incarceration. Since the industrial revolution, disabled (and often elderly) people had been segregated in institutions which were frequently out of town and out of sight. Former workhouses were turned into hospitals and residential institutions for a variety of people. Despite the fact that comparatively few people had ever been admitted to workhouses, their negative image endured and those who were forced to live in such institutions – the mentally ill and the learning disabled – consequently suffered. Not all institutions were harsh and repressive with an adverse impact on the lives of the residents, but most suffered from public attitudes and assumptions that were the legacies of their origins, namely that the residents were frequently neglected and often dangerous.

The Guillebaud Report of 1956 acknowledged the long-standing concern within central government about the high and rising costs of hospital provision. Throughout the 1970s, pressure groups such as MIND and MENCAP argued the case for a total rethink about hospital-based provision, and gradually won support from academics and practitioners. Two White Papers in 1971 and 1975 argued for the abandoning of hospitals to provide better services for the learning disabled and the mentally ill. A Report by the King's Fund in 1980, *An Ordinary Life*, stressed three fundamental principles in its argument for comprehensive, locally based services for 'mentally handicapped' people. These were the recognition that those with learning disability had the same human value as anyone else and were therefore entitled to the same human rights. This gave them the right to live in the community like other people. The report recognised that this was more than a right; it was a need. Finally, the report argued that services should recognise the individuality of handicapped people and cater accordingly. Simultaneously, there was growing concern about basic standards of care in the hospitals. When this was fuelled by press interest into allegations of ill-treatment and abuse, another policy response was forced. The NHS Reorganisation Act of 1973 established new planning machinery, and was followed by the introduction of joint finance in 1976. Under these terms, social services departments could for a limited period obtain health authority money which might aid in the hospital reprovision programme or provide support for people to remain in the community.

Pressure for reform built up during the 1980s. A consultative document, *Care in the Community* (1981), contained some radical proposals, but the subsequent *Care in the Community and Joint Finance* (1983) adopted a less imaginative approach, confirming that Care in the Community was not top of the government's agenda. Private nursing and residential homes (mainly for the elderly) sprang up in the mid-1980s, but some health authorities were using the private sector as an alternative source of accommodation for patients from mental handicap institutions. There was, however, high level official criticism of the failure to develop community care policies. The House of Commons Social Services Select Committee concluded in 1985 that despite the bias towards getting people out of hospital, most people with special needs were being cared for already in the community, by their families. There was little consensus on what good practice in community care was, but the Committee did argue that it should be based on ordinary housing. The Committee also highlighted the accelerating pace of running down the hospitals before adequate community-based services were in place and the need for an increase in total resources to ensure that the services were not understaffed or underresourced. It also advocated responsiveness to user preferences. The initial response was frustrating, but the following year the Audit Commission produced *Making a Reality of Community Care* (1986) which concluded that the implementation of community care had been slow, unevenly successful across the country and that too many people had been moved from large institutions to small ones (nursing or residential homes) rather than into genuine community-based arrangements. They did, however, note that some good local community care schemes were developing, in spite of the shortcomings of the existing system. They identified the successful projects as those where there was a dedicated local advocate of these innovations, where action was prioritised, where services were integrated locally rather than restricted to competing agencies, and where there was a neighbourhood focus and a multidisciplinary approach. Fundamentally, the Audit Commission recognised the necessity of profound and strategic change.

The government's response was swift. It asked Sir Roy Griffiths to undertake a brief but action-oriented report. St Anne's was one of the voluntary organisations Sir Roy visited during his investigations. He noted the government's failure to link the objectives of community care policy to the available resources, and the frequent muddles at local level where health, social services and housing authorities, and the voluntary and private sectors were failing to coordinate. He concluded that there should be a mixed economy of social care provision, where statutory, private and voluntary sectors competed on an equal footing and that the current subsidising of private and voluntary sector nursing home places was wasteful. He proposed that the government appoint a Minister of Community Care and that social services departments should play the leading role in identifying local community care needs and coordinating services. He suggested that housing authority involvement should be restricted to the physical provision of community care and not be involved in the delivery of care. He then turned to health authorities, advancing the view that they should only be responsible for medically required community care, while general medical practitioners should keep their local social services departments informed about the needs of their patients for non-health care. He further proposed that there should be an assessment of financial means and of care needs for all residents of residential and nursing homes and finally that individuals should be expected to plan ahead to meet their social and community care needs, especially those of old age.

There was a mixed reaction to this report. Critics questioned Griffiths's assumptions about the ability of people to pay for their social care needs, his failure to address the role and burden put on informal carers, his marginalisation of housing and the confident prediction that further growth of a service delivery role for the private sector would be unproblematic. On the positive side, the report avoided another massive reorganisation and underlined a commitment to local government. It also defined the responsibilities of central government and stressed the need for local leadership.

This report, *Community Care: An Agenda for Action* (1988), was followed by a White Paper in 1989. Its recommendations were that market mechanisms should be used wherever possible. This would establish competition between providers which would in turn promote efficiency, choice and a customer orientation. It advocated that individual choice should take precedence over collective choices and planned provision, and finally that state provision should be kept to a minimum. This meant that the state should cease to be both the funder and the provider of care services, and become merely the funder, with the services provided by a variety of private, voluntary and public suppliers, all operating in competition in a 'quasi-market.' This led to the National Health Service and Community Care Act 1990.

The multiplicity and heterogeneity of the many variables in community care risk being simplified in these very broad generalisations, and the story is

still playing out. The 1990s have been difficult for social services departments, and these difficulties cascade on to the providers. They have had to
implement the internal market with its purchaser–provider splits in a period
of political uncertainty. Initially some Labour-controlled authorities dragged
their feet on restructuring, hoping for a change of government in 1992. The
collapse of the Poll Tax and the difficulties of introducing the new Council
Tax resulted in financial stringency, which was intensified by the government's attempts to control public expenditure and local authority spending.
This forced some local authorities to cut their budgets. Standard spending
assessments (SSAs) for social services were introduced in 1990/91. These
are the formulae by which the Department of the Environment calculates the
amount of money an authority needs to spend on personal social services.
They were divided into three blocks – children (35.5%), elderly people
(45.2%) and adults requiring support (19.3%). Adults with special needs had
to be catered for out of the smallest segment, which not surprisingly was
criticised as inadequate, and with unjustifiable regional variations. The 1990
Act had been preceded by the Children Act 1989, which exacerbated the
problems created by the sheer volume of new legislation and change. These
two vital and complex pieces of legislation also embodied different and
sometimes conflicting approaches to social work, thus compounding the difficulties these departments faced. These difficulties have led to suggestions of
even more organisational restructuring to meet these divergent demands.
Further uncertainty hung over local authorities until the review of local government boundaries was completed. Difficulties and uncertainties faced by
the purchaser led to insecurities and uncertainties on the part of the service
providers, who constantly had to readjust to meet the new situation. This in
itself mitigates against optimum care for those in nursing or residential care,
as growth, developments and extensions to the service are unlikely to be
possible.

The 1990s also saw the implementation of care management systems and
needs-led assessments. The policy guidance issued by the Department of
Health in 1990 described the stages of proper care management as an assessment of a user's circumstances, the negotiation of a care package which was
designed to meet these identified needs within obtainable resources, and the
implementation and review of the agreed package. The policy guidance
argued that the new system, being needs-led, would overcome the shortcomings in the existing arrangements and achieve significant objectives. These
included the effective use of resources to meet individual needs, enabling

people to live as independent a life as possible within the community, mini-mising the effects of disability, providing equal opportunities for all by treat-ing service users with respect, promoting individual choice and finally promoting partnership between users, carers and service providers.

Social services departments were responsible to the local authority to cre-ate a market in social care by maximising the service delivery role of the vol-untary and private sectors. They were also expected to expand this market from residential care to the provision of domiciliary services, where so far the market is far less developed. Chapters in this volume will examine the extent to which this has taken place, suggest future trends and recommend some approaches which will ensure the best possible services reach some of the most vulnerable people in our society.

The history of St Anne's is deliberately narrative. It is aimed at staff and volunteers in similar organisations as much as academics and managers. There is a considerable literature on community care and housing issues which too easily sanitise the passion, belief and commitment that an organi-sation such as St Anne's needs to drive it forward. The background informa-tion in this introduction and several other chapters can easily be juxtaposed with the chronological framework by the more clinical reader.

Gerald Wistow begins by looking back at the world into which St Anne's was born when anything other than 'the continuing dominance and growth' of the state welfare model was inconceivable. He also addresses the problems created by cuts in public spending and the introduction of a social care mar-ket and reflects on some of the debates which have informed the develop-ment of community care policy since 1971. He maintains that it is critical that payment systems do not subsume the service principles underlying the community care policy; that it is imperative not to mistake the management of dependence for the promotion of independence; and that housing under-pins both community care and its successful realisation. He concludes with the warning that neither the state nor the market can guarantee the funding that is now expected for social care, and urges a new social contract which is less exposed to assaults from either party.

By focusing on St Anne's 'Statement of values and beliefs' Alan Butler illustrates changing attitudes in the field of mental health. He too examines the historical context, and concentrates on four main areas – medication, housing, normalisation and empowerment, and quality of life – establishing their interrelationship and the organisation's response to evolving theory and practice.

In examining quality of life issues Nigel Malin has drawn heavily on observations and data supplied by St Anne's care staff on changes in the residents since they moved from institutional to community care. These remarks seem overwhelmingly positive. The indicators can be codified but are rarely given formal recognition or used as a measure of the impact of successful community care on the lifestyle of individuals. However they enhance choice and independence, which remain core aims of residential services. He delivers a timely warning against complacency in residential services for people with learning disabilities, as there is no national data on the way such units are managed, the successes and disappointments, or on the users' experiences, and suggests that systematic research on this topic might draw clear distinctions between the users' preferences and staff perceptions of their improved quality of life.

Alan Deacon brings us back to St Anne's origins in providing for single homeless people. Increasingly, work in St Anne's services for homeless people is more about resettlement and less about crisis management and the maintaining of homeless people in that lifestyle. He calls for a range of provision for single homeless people, including group homes, supported special needs housing and independent houses and flats. He also reminds us that it is crucial to retain some direct access provision to meet the needs of both the newly homeless and those who have decided to continue to travel. His scenario matches the services St Anne's provides, namely a direct access hostel (in Sheffield), a resettlement hostel (in Leeds), and supported special needs housing. The essence is to give homeless people choices which both meet their needs and satisfy their aspirations.

One test of community care will be the experience of people with special needs from black or ethnic minority groups. It may be possible to access culturally sensitive services in major towns where there are large ethnic minority populations, but this may not always be the case where the majority of the population is white. St Anne's has recently launched a research and development project to assess the barriers to entering mainstream provision which people from ethnic minorities find, and to assess how special needs provision can be extended to encompass the whole community. Ian Law and colleagues deal particularly with youth homelessness amongst black and minority ethnic communities. These young people are disproportionately represented among those vulnerable to homelessness and face particularly serious problems, yet the provision they preferred – black-led hostel accommodation – is still relatively scarce. Like Alan Deacon, Ian Law and his colleagues conclude that a range of provision is crucial, as is a machinery to coordinate it, and that black-led projects should be fully integrated into projects catering for young homeless people, and not regarded as specialist or marginal.

Janet Ford examines trends in employment and the impact of labour market change on owner-occupation, and in turn on social housing. This has the potential for repercussions on to the community care sector as those who could no longer sustain owner-occupation may now require social housing, and tenants in social housing are experiencing unemployment, loss of employment, low pay or work disincentives. She forecasts an important and ongoing role for housing associations, albeit a problematic one.

Finally, Mike Blackburn gives us the view of the commercial lender in regard to owner-occupation, social renting and private renting. He predicts an interesting and varied role for lenders, who, with capital assistance from government, could help tackle the problems of urban decay and social deprivation in the inner cities. He recognises the need to improve and sustain both the quality and the quantity of the housing stock into the next century and even foresees the possibility of large, responsible corporate landlords. These may be the big financial institutions themselves if government help is forthcoming. The reassurance that the Halifax is prepared to play its part in the fight against social exclusion ends the volume on an optimistic note.

This volume has looked at some of the aspects of housing and community care which confront St Anne's. It has been an attempt to pay tribute to an innovative and successful organisation whose name is a byword for high standards in all the services it provides. Survival and growth have been the result of determination, foresight and opportunism, and an ability to read the signs and keep ahead of the game. The persistent quest to maintain and improve services despite changes in legislation, policy, funding and fortunes must encourage residents, tenants, attenders and families that St Anne's will continue to be a leader in imagination and excellence in the provision of services for homeless people or those with special needs.

References

Audit Commission (1986) *Making a Reality of Community Care.* London: HMSO.

Department of Health and Social Security (1981) *Care in the Community: A Consultative Document on Moving Resources for Care in England.* London: DHS.

Department of Health and Social Security (1983) *Care in the Community and Joint Finance,* Health circular (83)6 and Local Authority Circular (83)5 London: DHSS.

Griffiths, R. (1988) *Community Care: An Agenda for Action.* London: HMSO.King's Fund Centre (1980) *An Ordinary Life: Comprehensive Locally-based residential Services for Mentally Handicapped People.* King's Fund Project, Paper No 24. London: King's Fund.

CHAPTER I

The Rise of St Anne's Shelter and Housing Action

Pancrack to Pan-Yorkshire

Fiona Spiers

Every new member of staff at St Anne's faces 'basic training' – an induction not just into the current philosophy and practice of the organisation, but also into its history and development. As any organisation increasingly accepts its own mythology, this in turn influences current attitudes. Trustees, staff and supporters live with an 'authorised version' which subtly informs their perception of where their organisation came from, the forces that shaped it, and where it is heading. This account relates the amazing growth of the organisation from a small group of volunteers in borrowed premises to a substantial organisation of 720 staff working at numerous sites throughout Yorkshire, from Ripon to Sheffield and from Todmorden to York, making the growth appear both logical and inevitable. The problem for the historian is unravelling this interaction between mythology and actuality, where few documents remain from the early years and where the folk memory is still a potent source. Several interwoven strands need to be untangled to explain why this organisation not only survived but grew to become one of the top 200 charities in the country. These include the motivation of the founders and subsequent leaders; the relationship with the local Roman Catholic Church; the development of social services; the creation of other homeless charities nationally; and the organisation's interaction with local and health authorities. Throughout its history St Anne's has also had an evolving relationship with its client groups, which in turn has influenced the directions it has taken.

Charities usually start small, concentrating on a particular problem or in one geographical area. They usually come about when people see a need they wish to address, or feel a need themselves for which they want support. The late 1960s had seen a mushrooming of pressure and support groups, both informal and formal, which focused on very precise categories of social or physical conditions (Cooper, 1983). In the early 1960s the publicity surrounding the notorious landlord Peter Rachman made the nation aware of terrible housing conditions. The birth of Shelter in the wake of interest aroused by Jeremy Sandford's *Cathy Come Home* created pioneering and hard-hitting campaigns on the issues of housing and homelessness. Slowly the public came to accept the fact that there were many more homeless people than were officially acknowledged, although the cities where 'acute need' was identified were London, Glasgow, Birmingham and Liverpool (Shelter, 1996). In 1969 Leeds had been shamed when the body of a Nigerian vagrant David Oluwale was found in the River Aire. His death aroused considerable public concern, led to the prosecution of two policemen and was infamous enough to be the subject of a second Sandford play in 1972 (Sandford, 1974).

By early 1971, a number of people had voiced their concern at the plight of homeless people gathering around St Anne's Cathedral, Leeds. This was at a time when the Catholic Church was developing a new structure including an Area Pastoral Council at which representatives of the Catholic parishes and organisations came together. At a meeting in March 1971, the attention of this group was drawn to the problems of homeless people, particularly single homeless men. Both priests and lay people expressed concern at the numbers of men calling on churches for help and using city centre churches for refuge during the day. The Leeds Area Pastoral Council called a public meeting in April and three people, Father Neil Gallanagh, Mr John Hemingway and Father Bill Kilgallon were asked to conduct a survey and bring recommendations to the Council (St Anne's Shelter & Housing Action First Annual Report, 1972).

The survey was conducted by Kilgallon, who, in addition to examining the existing services offering night accommodation and discussing the situation with local statutory and voluntary agencies involved in this work, also actually interviewed the homeless people themselves. 'User consultation' is now taken for granted in present-day good practice; in 1971 it was considered radical. Instinct rather than theory guided the initial impetus, but it set the tone for the way St Anne's would operate – responsiveness to client need in combination with partnership and cooperation with other agencies.

It was clear fairly quickly that the overpowering need was for daytime provision. There was a sufficient number of night shelters in Leeds at the time, including the Church Army hostel, the Salvation Army hostel, St George's Crypt, Shaftesbury House and The Grove (Annual Report, 1972; *Yorkshire Evening Post*, 1971). All compelled residents to leave the building during the day, condemning them to roam the streets and find shelter as best they could. Such homeless people would call at Cathedral House, looking for a hot drink, a seat in the cathedral where they could keep warm and dry and possibly for company. The group recommended a day shelter be opened, and the Council agreed to support the project. The project had an auspicious beginning as the administrator of the cathedral – Mgr Tom Murphy – agreed to make space available. With this prospect of accommodation, there was no loss of momentum and enthusiasm. One of the major factors driving the project forward was the dedication of Father Kilgallon. His duties as priest allowed him time to develop the project, and then later to run it, and his role provided access to volunteers and resources. All the furniture and equipment was begged or donated, and with a scant regard for planning permission the room was divided to provide toilets at one end and a kitchen at the other, with the main part of the room being laid out like a cafe with tables and chairs. Sixth formers from St Thomas Aquinas Grammar School and Notre Dame Grammar School gave up their time over the summer holidays to clear out the disused rooms where the conversion was planned, and Chris Clair, an architect who is to this day a member of the Council of Management, drew up the basic design. In November and December 1971 the *Yorkshire Evening Post* had run a series of features on 'The Dossers' and had galvanised public sympathy. The shelter opened on Saturday 4 December 1971 and, after all the effort, only 12 people turned up. However, word spread rapidly and the following day over 80 people arrived. There were not enough cups and plates for everyone. The numbers stabilised throughout 1972 and have retained a similar pattern over a quarter of a century, with fluctuations between 40 and 235 (Day Book, 1972; Allinson (1985); Attenders' Surveys, 1992, 1993, 1994, 1995).

The original group who ran the shelter were self-selecting, brought together by their shared commitment and willingness to mitigate the circumstances of the homeless people they encountered on the streets. Help and interest came from a wide spectrum of people. Sally Trench, the author who had lived rough to write *Bury Me in My Boots* in 'Black Like Me' style, took an early interest, introducing her caretaker, Jem Roche to the group. Jem started to work at the shelter in December 1971, shortly after it opened. By that time he was already in his 70s. He had been born in Ireland of a very well established family with substantial retail interests. He had served in the Irish army as an officer, but had become an alcoholic and a drifter. He had come to Yorkshire to work with Sally Trench at a house she was setting up in Chapeltown. A large man, Roche had retained his upright bearing and military style, an image confirmed by his old-fashioned moustache. He had great aplomb, and a real empathy with those who used the shelter. His vast experience, loyalty and devotion to the cause, and mischievous sense of humour, set a welcoming tone. His informal 'no names, no packdrill' approach still persists today in the open-door policy of the day centre.

Initially the shelter opened every day of the week, from 8.00am to 6.00pm. It was exactly what its name implied – a daytime shelter for those in need. Simple meals, for example bread and soup, were served free of charge. The aim was to provide a 'friendly, accepting atmosphere where homeless men could come and go freely without pressure' (Annual Report, 1972). The shelter was run by full-time volunteers who worked for rent, board and a little pocket money, effectively placing them in the same financial position as the men using the shelter. This movement of people who wished to help 'down and outs' provided a ready source of volunteers. Their dedication to the cause is evidenced by the working conditions in which they persevered not only without complaint but with commendable good humour. The day books record the wry wit of Jem Roche and others even when confronted by severe tribulation, but they cannot recapture the smells of inadequate drainage systems, people who had nowhere to take care of their personal hygiene and vast pots of vegetables on their way to becoming soup. The grim working conditions with 'the smell of poverty' never dampened their commitment (Interview with T. Ryan, 1996).

Even from the early days there was a gap between the organisation's image and the reality of the way it was run. While many of the workers and volunteers believed that God would provide (Interview with C. Clair, 1997), Kilgallon was out systematically securing funds. This continued for several years. Tony Ryan, the social worker at the shelter from 1974 to 1976, remembers the project as being 'very Christian based ... We didn't worry about money ... it just came in'. He saw his work as 'meeting the suffering Christ every day' (Interview 1996). In the first year, donations had come predominantly though the Church – from priests, parishes, convents and nuns, or from the Bishop's Fund (Annual Report, 1972). By 1973, to the surprise of the organisation, much of this support had waned, despite the fact that the organisation had originated in the Leeds Area Pastoral Council which represented the parishes and Catholic societies of the city. Running costs had spiralled from £3217 per annum for the first year of operation to over £15,000 per annum and, despite help from the Bishop of Leeds, the organisation had to turn to the city council, the Department of Health and Social Security, charitable trusts and 'an expensive friend' – the local bank manager (Annual Report, 1973, pp.26–7). The Church had many other demands on its charity and resources, while the organisation needed to diversify its sources of income to survive and grow. Even before the shelter relocated to Bingley Street in 1973, the secularisation of the organisation had begun.

St Anne's had a conception typical of many voluntary organisations. Frequently only two volunteers were there to staff it. Those who founded the organisation had such zeal and commitment that they were prepared to exploit themselves for the good of others to ensure the success of their endeavour. This is chronicled in the day book for 1972, which details how frequently there were only two volunteers on duty, and how often Father Kilgallon ran the shelter single-handed. This commitment meant that the difficulties were minimised and overcome.

Belief, instinct and experience guided the founding principles at a time when there were very few other day centres from which to seek advice on good practice. Never having seen a day centre, they were without a model. Kilgallon and Roche set about drafting a minimal policy to make the centre safe and welcoming. The rules were kept few and simple: 'No Violence' and 'No Drink'. They wanted homeless people to be able to access shelter without let or hindrance, to be able to feel that this was 'their place' where the staff were only present to help find accommodation and to give advice. These latter aspects distinguished St Anne's from a soup kitchen, for although food was dispensed, the aim of the centre was to be proactive rather than palliative.

A fairly robust attitude was taken to any outbreaks of violence. The 1972 day book lists every 'Pancrack Day' when benefit was paid, to alert staff to possible trouble as the users spent their allowances on drink. The activities of the 'surgers' (people who drank surgical spirit) are also recorded. The ex-military man knew the ropes, and his size was a deterrent despite his age. The priest was protected by his collar and a status enhanced by some early successful results against some of the hard men. The third member of staff – Theresa Tracey – was protected by her sex and her peace-making skills (interview with Bill Kilgallon, 1996). The police were always supportive in days when there was much more of a city centre neighbourhood than one might imagine – a camaraderie shared by police, clergymen, nurses and care-takers. This good relationship with the police still endures.

Kilgallon was quickly aware that a new service had been created, and optimistically believed that all the homeless could be rehoused in a matter of a few years. On Boxing Day 1971 he travelled to London to look at day cen-tres in St Martin's in the Fields and St Botolph's. While in the capital he stayed at Marlyebone church house. Another guest was a Passionist monk who was then studying at the LSE, Father Paulinus Healy.

Healy was the only child of devout Catholic immigrants who worked in the Batley textile mills. Educated in Belfast and Dublin, he was ordained in 1952. He had worked in Glasgow with street drinkers and in Soho with pimps and prostitutes but had decided that a formal training in social work would give him an advantage over other clerics who tried to help society's unfortunates (*Batley Reporter*, 1992). He was attracted to the course which offered placements in alcohol projects at the Maudsley and Rathcoole House. Kilgallon knew that here was someone who could help drive his organisation on, and he invited Healy to come to Leeds on graduating the following September. This invitation was issued on his own initiative, not in consultation with the group in Leeds, but with a drive born of supreme confi-dence in his own ability to make things happen and by faith in the unstoppa-ble justice of his project. In order to ensure Healy took the bait, Kilgallon also promised that by the time he arrived in Leeds nine months later, St Anne's would already own its first house.

The day-to-day running of the shelter continued as the organisation took on a more formal aspect. The group formed itself into a management com-mittee, which Bill Kilgallon chaired, and the organisation took the name, designed by committee, of 'St Anne's Shelter & Housing Action'. The name was designed to reflect where they were, what they did and the commitment to do more than talk. A company and a charity were formed and the founda-tions for a more permanent organisation were laid. Within one year the group had launched a campaign of public education, established a network of key contacts throughout the city and started to liaise with national bodies in the same field (Annual Report, 1973).

The first annual report alludes to this aim of educating the public about homelessness, with staff speaking in schools, parishes and to community groups. Aware that homelessness was a national issue, the committee acknowledged a debt to pioneering work done by other organisations, principally the Cyrenians. St Anne's had also joined the National Association of Voluntary Hostels and applied for membership of the National Association for Mental Health and the National Association for the Care and Resettlement of Offenders. The contacts forged with the public health and social service departments of the local authority, the social services committee, the police and the Leeds Council for Social Service (Healy, 1975) served notice that this was more than a group of altruistic philanthropists; it was a group with political antennae, a wide perspective and a ruthless ambition to do its best for its users.

Kilgallon now had to deliver on his promise to Healy. The decision to buy the house was ratified; the only problem was raising the money. After every building society had turned him down, and with a property at 40 Kelso Road in mind, Kilgallon eventually managed to persuade the diocesan treasurer, Canon Ted Wilcox, to make the advance of £5,000 for the property and £500 to furnish it. As emergency overnight accommodation in Leeds was deemed to be adequate, in consultation with Healy it was decided to make the house a community for recovering alcoholics. It became home to 12 men, as well as Healy himself. The intention had been to open the house early in 1973, but the government had issued Circular 21/73, *Community Services for Alcoholics*, in that year, so opening was delayed in order that this house could be among the first to benefit from that funding. Pragmatism and the harsh realities of funding were shaping the programme and determining the timetable, but access to government funding enabled the organisation to repay the diocese, and proved that the organisation could use money shrewdly.

The shift in leadership from Kilgallon to Healy changed the tone and focus of the organisation. Kilgallon still had parochial responsibilities, and was devoting his energies to fundraising, talks and raising his own awareness of the national scene. Healy was charismatic, a brilliant orator who could lift any audience with his obvious commitment and idealism. He quickly became authoritative and known in the trade for his work with homeless drinkers, being invited to be a member of the government's review of alcohol services headed by Professor Neil Kessel. Healy was a keen networker and knew all the key players on the national scene (which admittedly was not large) and more importantly he knew key people in social administration who were

about to become advisers to the Labour government. He was, however, cha-
otically disorganised with no grasp of the administration for which he was
employed, a shortcoming which would prove his undoing.

Certain changes were already underway before Healy arrived in Leeds. It
became obvious fairly quickly that the original premises were too small, as
they became congested at various times during the day. Talks began with
Leeds city council in 1972 to see if they could help. A surprise visit one
Sunday from the chairman of the social services committee, Bill Merritt,
resulted in an agreement by the council to make a grant and help find new
premises. After negotiations led by Kilgallon and Healy, St Anne's Day Shelter moved out of the Cathedral and into Bingley Street which the council
provided at a peppercorn rent. This was a less central location but that did not
lessen the numbers coming to the shelter. The new premises offered scope to
increase the involvement of the men in the life of the shelter and opportunities to branch out into new ways of help and self-help. There were plans to
offer workshop and work schemes and to increase the level of social work
support (Annual Report, 1973).

The organisation had now grown to a point where it provided two dis-
tinct services, and the Council of Management decided professional management was needed for both projects. Management committees were formed
for both the day shelter and for St Anne's House (as Kelso Road had been
named), and included representatives from the probation service and Leeds
social services department, medical advisers and psychiatrists. It is important
to note that a resident was also elected to the management committee of St
Anne's House. Kilgallon chaired the Council of Management and the two
subcommittees, but was pulling back from the day-to-day administration
which was left to Healy.

In September 1974 Bill Kilgallon left Leeds to study social work, first at
the London School of Economics and then at Warwick, where he helped
establish a day centre in Coventry as part of his postgraduate studies. St
Anne's was now entirely controlled by Healy, who was principally interested
in developing services for alcoholics. The origins of the detoxification centre
can be found in T.G. Weiler's report for the Home Office, *Habitual Drunken
Offenders*, published in 1971. Healy's marginalia confirm his endorsement of
the working party's conclusions. Public drunkenness had increased
dramatically during the 1960s, which is why the Home Secretary had
commisioned a working party to investigate suitable alternatives to prison for
habitual drunkenness offenders. Healy welcomed the proposed estab-

lishment of detoxification centres. (Healy, 1975). The significant shift of responsibility for drunken offenders from the Home Office to the DHSS also marked a changing emphasis from punishment to treatment. The government was recognising that this was a public health problem that should be dealt with as a partnership between relevant statutory and voluntary authorities. The statutory services had the responsibility, but alcoholics were more likely to respond to the approach offered in a non-statutory setting. The Criminal Justice Act of 1972 enabled police to take a drunkenness offender to a detoxification centre instead of charging him, and it was envisaged that a small number of these experimental centres would be established in cities where the need had been demonstrated. Leeds, with the second highest rate of drunkenness in the country having 70.89 drunkenness arrests per 10,000 population in 1970, was an obvious candidate. Healy envisaged his detoxification centre (his 'detox') as a first-aid rescue centre from which the patient would move on to a diagnostic (social and medical) and allocation centre. It would be a point at which all services available to the alcoholic converged. There were obvious advantages to the patients who would be able to access integrated and appropriate care, to the hospital services whose casualty departments often had difficulties meeting the demands of homeless alcoholics and who would no longer have to admit them, and to the judicial system who would no longer have to process and prosecute them (Healy, 1975).

Healy set about a comprehensive strategy to 'win' a detox. He established cooperation and partnerships with the DHSS, the police, the local authority, the area health authority, won the backing of Sir Keith Joseph, and then set up a working party of all relevant agencies. Premises were obtained – St Mark's House – where a specially trained staff would be based. Alcoholics are supportive of one another if in a 'client-orientated therapeutic community environment' and this self-help and mutual aid were to be built into the programme. It was also recognised that this treatment was voluntary and that there was no compulsion; people were free to leave at any time. St Mark's was in an ideal location as it was close to the area where most arrests were made, near to Leeds General Infirmary and other relevant agencies, surrounded by university property where there were few neighbours to object, although parents and governors at Notre Dame Grammar School had required some reassurance, and it could cater for approximately 15 men which was regarded as a desirable size. The police were involved and cooperative from the beginning. Their support and the active concern of the city council, whose director and chairman of social services located the premises, ensured that St Anne's opened this country's first community-based detoxification service in 1976.

St Anne's was now providing two essential services in Leeds – a day centre for homeless people and a detoxification centre and house for recovering alcoholics. The committee structures had become much more permanent, trustees (known as Council of Management members) included experts from a wide range of fields, and the sources of funding had also diversified. Much of the funding now came from grants from the statutory authorities, and the need for traditional community-based fundraising waned. Cooperation with other voluntary organisations was actively encouraged, as for example in 1975 when St Anne's was one of the founder members of Leeds Federated Housing Association.

In the Healy years St Anne's was known for its alcohol services. Healy insisted that St Anne's should be viewed as an experimental project, where ideas are generated and their validity tested. This was his legacy to the organisation. He was able to consolidate an organisation which recognised and valued social work and professional training, where an interest in research led to the development of new projects, and which worked in very close partnership with all other relevant agencies. He had also established a series of after-care houses and a day support centre for problem drinkers. He continued the beliefs and commitment of St Anne's founders, and forged the organisation's reputation locally and nationally for being at the cutting edge of new service provision.

The new service required new staff. Tony Ryan moved from the day shelter to the detox when it opened in 1976, and a financial administrator, Roy Simmons, was appointed. Ryan's successor at the centre ran away on his first day (a telling reminder of how volatile a workplace a day centre can be), and the job was advertised. There was only one applicant – Bill Kilgallon, who was back in Leeds after completing his studies. On his return, he had been appointed to the Catholic Children's Society by the Bishop, but he was quick to take the opportunity to return to St Anne's which this vacancy offered. Kilgallon returned to St Anne's in February 1977. Relations quickly became tense and strained between the director and founder: the director owed his job and status to the founder, who was now his employee. Neither were comfortable with these newly reversed roles (interview with Kilgallon, 1996). Healy had changed considerably from the genial man who had arrived in 1973. Unknown to those who appointed him, his interest in alcoholism stemmed from his own unresolved problems. He had made an initial recovery from alcoholism, but had had no support mechanisms to sustain him, and 'broke out' again around the time the detox opened (interview with Ryan, 1996). He was also afraid that Kilgallon had returned to take back the organisation.

After a complaint from Healy's former secretary, a council member started an investigation and demanded an audit, as a result of which Healy and Simmons were brought in for questioning. Both were sacked. Healy speedily departed for Canada. Simmons threw nearly every document and financial record on a bonfire, and was later arrested and tried for fraud. Unworldly and negligent rather than criminal, Healy nevertheless felt responsible.

The organisation was severely shaken internally by these events, but there were no public repercussions. The Leeds courts were so overcrowded that the trial was held in Knaresborough, so the scandal never featured in the local media. However, it highlighted the importance of establishing disciplinary and grievance procedures, of proper accounting procedures and of ensuring that the trustees really did hold the staff accountable. In August 1978 the Council of Management appointed Kilgallon Acting Director while the job was advertised nationally. The following month he was confirmed in post and began the task of redesigning the organisation's structure. The Founding Father had regained control, but this time he was confronted with an entirely different challenge.

The world had moved on from the heady days of 1971. Neither Healy's abrupt departure nor Kilgallon's resignation in 1977 from the clergy for personal reasons (which had excited considerable local newspaper interest) had caused a rift with the Catholic Church, but by 1978 the secularisation of St Anne's, which had started with the diversification of funding sources as early as 1973, was complete. There were no longer any clergy on the staff. The Catholic Church and its members continued their generous support, but any official connection had dissolved.

In the 1977 Housing (Homeless Persons) Act, homelessness had been legally recognised as a housing issue for the first time, having previously been dealt with as a welfare issue under the 1948 National Assistance Act. This Act, later incorporated into the 1985 Housing Act, gave certain categories of homeless people the right to rehousing. These changes had a significant impact on the climate in which St Anne's operated and on its perception of itself, and the organisation was delighted by the real benefits brought about by these improvements. Social service departments of local authorities had come into being with the 1971 implementation of the Seebohm Report.

Local authority housing departments were then the dominant supplier of accommodation services, but already there was a realisation that non-statutory, not-for-profit organisations would be moving into this type of service provision, especially for people who had previously been resident in long-stay hospitals.

By 1978 St Anne's was virtually reliant on statutory funding. It was entering a period of rapid growth and a time when there was considerable uncertainty over the funding of its existing services (Annual Report, 1979–80). Kilgallon had returned to a much more complex organisation with the benefits and the baggage of a social work training, but with his energy and determination if anything reinforced. An attempt to replace instinct and charisma with rules and accountability seemed overdue. Whereas the latter were scrupulously introduced to make St Anne's a model of good practice in its fields, the achievements and survival of the organisation can be partially ascribed to the fact that it never successfully divested itself of a charismatic leadership. It has therefore kept an identity, a direction and a sense of purpose which distinguishes it from more anonymous organisations.

The needs of another group of homeless people had now been identified in the day centre. Mental health pressure groups were winning the arguments against hospital-based provision, and the government White Papers of 1971 and 1975 agreed that better services could be provided in the community. The advent of new drugs and treatments also meant that mentally ill people could be catered for in a community setting. In 1977, St Anne's sponsored research into the needs of people with mental health problems. The research, by Maurice Ziff, recommended that St Anne's enter into partnership with the social service department to provide community-based after-care facilities for homeless people with mental health problems. These would be developed over a period of five years, with capital, revenue and deficit costs provided through Leeds Housing Federated (sic) and staffing funded through Joint Financing. (Healy, 1977) At the time, Joint Financing was seen as a radical initiative which allowed health funds to be spent outside the National Health Service. St Anne's was one of the earliest recipients of this, and the foundations were then laid for future NHS-linked work. The first of these properties, Oak Lodge (now known as Rowanbank) opened in 1978. This development at St Anne's predated The King's Fund report by two years.

In 1979 the detox faced a funding crisis. The scheme had only really got started in Leeds and Manchester, and the prospects of further centres looked remote. The initial three-year funding from the DHSS, who expected responsibility to pass to local funders, was about to expire. A six-month extension then four months support by the Inner City Fund completed the financial year, and allowed sufficient time for St Anne's to put together a funding consortium which reflected the fact that the service offered related to the work of a variety of statutory agencies. This funding consortium comprised Leeds area health authority, Leeds city council, the Home Office and the West Yorkshire police authority (Annual Report, 1979–80).

With this crisis safely over, St Anne's entered a period of simultaneously consolidating its new administrative structures and continuing to broaden its activities. In 1981 it registered as a housing association, which allowed it access to a housing association grant (HAG) for capital development in its own right. This new opportunity enabled St Anne's to make direct provision for people with special housing needs, which was key to evolving such a diverse range of services. At first there had been some resistance to this move, as in order to register it was necessary to meet the Housing Corporation's strict criteria. But, with the changes in funding for alcohol services necessitated by the ending of funding from Circular 21/73 the only way of housing homeless drinkers seemed to be through housing associations. Registration also allowed access to revenue funding from the Housing Corporation. The Housing Corporation was keen that St Anne's should register, and this was put through very quickly for 1 April 1981 (Annual Report, 1980–81).

From the mid-1970s St Anne's had been involved in job creation programmes and had run workshops from St Anne's Shelter. In 1982 St Anne's registered to run Community Programme, a programme established to give people work with pay for tasks which benefited the community. The initial scheme used the experience from the workshops to develop an entirely new project. Kilgallon's motivation in espousing the programme was not financial; he and Gordon Costello, recruited in 1983 to run the programme, believed they could provide a service from the workshops both to homeless people and to other charities, while at the same time giving the client group something to do. The furniture made in the workshops was affordable for homeless people, and it was of a decent quality as no compromises were made on standards (interview with G. Costello, 1996). The fact that money changed hands created a cash flow which was put to providing a bigger and better service.

The workshops themselves were a joint promotion with the probation service, with whom St Anne's was working to develop a policy of employment, which would recruit one-third of its participants from St Anne's clients, (i.e. homeless people or those with alcohol problems or mental ill health), one-third from probation and the final third from other voluntary organisa- tions. The mix was potentially explosive; there was no difficulty filling the first two quotas but the third group often failed. It was felt that work was beneficial to these client groups, as it would give a structure to their day while they regained old or lost skills. The building team helped St Anne's and many other charities undertake projects they could not otherwise have contem- plated. There were a separate set of ambitions for this team. St Anne's aimed to provide work experience rather than training for those who had been unemployed for a considerable time and to provide a service to a variety of client groups. Although operating on the fringe of commerciality, the schemes brought enormous benefits to not-for-profit organisations who without this service would not have been able to expand or improve their facilities. For example, Community Programme enabled a cricket club to pro- vide decent changing rooms; by using this source of labour a Sports Council grant could become adequate.

One of the major projects undertaken by this team was the renovation of the third St Anne's Centre. The roof at Bingley Street had eventually fallen in and new premises were a necessity. The building acquired on York Street had to be gutted and rebuilt, while attempts were made to make the conversion as low maintenance as possible to keep down future costs. The workshops were created on the ground floor of this building. In 1986, the shell of Head Office on its present site on St Mark's Avenue was ready to be fitted out by the building team. As income was generated it was applied to projects with maximum community benefit, many of which were St Anne's projects. In fact, without Community Programme St Anne's could not have embarked on all its undertakings of the mid-1980s. There was no question of profit; as the scheme was publicly funded it could only be used to enhance community services available in Leeds.

Employment Training was then introduced by the government to replace Community Programme, which entered a phase of orderly close down. In its six years of existence, it had encompassed a wide range of very imaginative schemes – furniture workshops, home care teams and building teams – which brought great benefit to the client groups and enabled St Anne's to establish much of the present infrastructure of the organisation (interview with Costello, 1996; Council of Management minutes 1986) Costello's business acumen brought home another valuable lesson to St Anne's, namely the need to create an asset backing. Each year the organisation used all its funds for the purposes for which they had been granted or donated, leaving it with few reserves at the end of each financial year. From the mid-1980s, St Anne's accepted the imperative of building up assets and reserves which would allow it the flexibility to do good works and survive future changes in government policy and funding. This was only fiscally prudent for an agency which was now the largest non-statutory social work organisation in the city.

The achievements of the Detox had not passed unnoticed on the Leeds magistrates bench. One magistrate, Mr Edwin Ashton, was so impressed with the centre's work that he offered to support the building of a new, totally separate treatment area to deal with admissions through his charitable trust. Ashton House, a purpose-built extension to St Mark's House, opened in 1984.

Nineteen-eighty-five was one of the organisation's busiest years. While the Detox was undergoing this major extension, St Anne's Centre completed the move to York Street, where it was able to offer a comprehensive social work and advice service in addition to basic facilities such as toilets, showers, laundry, food and activities (Annual Report, 1986; Council of Management minutes 1985). In addition to increasing numbers of homeless people with mental health problems, the centre had detected significant changes in the numbers and ages of homeless people. The numbers of young homeless people were noticeably growing, adding urgency to the need for specialist provision. Work on the new Head Office in St Mark's Avenue commenced with a close involvement from Community Programme and three key decisions were taken which would have a major influence on the organisation's future.

Up to this point, the growth of St Anne's had been against expectation, as its client group was generally regarded as low status and politically power-less. The development of the organisation was the result of a fortuitous com-bination of factors already noted: charismatic and determined leaders, the identification of changing and emerging client needs, opportunism and astuteness in accessing new sources of funding, the highly professional con-tributions of members of the Council of Management plus the use of external expertise, cooperation with other voluntary organisations and with the statu-tory sector, and a cordial relationship with the local authority. In the Introduction we noticed the escalation throughout the 1980s of the pressure for reform. The Audit Commission's 1986 report analysed the components of the successes in the implementation of community care. Their criteria were largely met by St Anne's, which partially explains St Anne's success. The services they were providing matched the most progressive thinking of the time.

Two factors which were to become increasingly important were the absence of any real competition and the successful political career Kilgallon carved out on Leeds city council from 1979 to 1992, which culminated in his election as Lord Mayor. Other agencies were not rushing to provide for these unpopular client groups and the close networking relationship St Anne's was carefully cultivating with the local and health authorities and with other agencies placed them in pole position to provide housing with support for vulnerable people. St Anne's was not in the right place at the right time by good luck; it made its own luck. It was ready to capitalise on each and every available opportunity for its clients by anticipating future needs and funding opportunities, and manœuvring to be ready to exploit these openings. St Anne's was growing at a time when voluntary organisations were taking on an increasing responsibility for the provision of residential and other social services. While still occasionally proactive, increasingly St Anne's preferred method of developing new services was to predict trends among purchasers and position itself accordingly. This was mutually beneficial while the organisation could provide a high quality service at an acceptable price.

The study *Single and Homeless* by the Department of the Environment concluded that the vast majority of single homeless people would prefer to be accommodated in mainstream accommodation, but that a significant minority required accommodation with support (DoE, 1983). Since its inception St Anne's had worked to access mainstream accommodation for its clients and to assist them to resettle. In 1985, it took the decision to provide 'fair rent' flats where there was a good standard of accommodation with an appropriate level of support for formerly homeless people, which would enhance their level of independence. The housing team, which included social work, care and management staff, opened two large converted houses in 1986 in accommodation which provided more privacy than group homes but less isolation than in independent tenancies (Annual Report, 1986: Council of Management minutes 1986). The introduction in 1982 of Housing Benefit, despite subsequent reductions in level, had enabled the development of this type of supported housing. It was seen as vital to foster good relationships between residents themselves and between residents and staff. A St Anne's Residents' Association was formed with this in view and received recognition and approval in a visit from the Lord Mayor (Annual Report 1986) This was yet another astute move as resettlement was becoming big business (Dant and Deacon, 1988) and paved the way to St Anne's becoming a major provider of supported tenancies to people with special needs.

In February 1985 the DHSS announced its intention to close 15 resettlement units, and St Anne's prepared again to be in a position to 'help' when needed. There was also a change in public perceptions of homelessness by the mid-1980s. During the 1960s concern with homelessness had centred on the plight of families; now public opinion at least partially recognised the problems of the single homeless (Dant and Deacon, 1988). The association between single homelessness and vagrancy was waning, and the belief that personal inadequacy was the root cause was supplanted by an understanding of the heterogeneous nature of the problem. With this increased understanding came an awareness that large hostels were inappropriate and damaging to those who lived there. This had already been grasped in Leeds some years previously when St Anne's and the Cyrenians, with the support of the housing department and the probation service, had established the Leeds Shaftesbury Project with precisely these aims. When St Anne's was able to offer its own supported accommodation, the Shaftesbury Project also benefited.

In 1983 Leeds city council and the health authorities had begun to develop policies for increasing community services to people with a learning disability (which was still called mental handicap at that time). In 1985 the Housing Corporation agreed to provide capital, and work began on four houses which St Anne's would manage for people with a learning disability. The first opened in 1987. St Anne's had started down the road which was to lead it to become Yorkshire's major provider of housing for people with learning disabilities. At the same time it took responsibility for its own development programme, thereby expanding its in-house expertise and removing its dependence on development agents.

In the same year another significant decision was taken; St Anne's accepted an invitation from Kirklees health and local authorities to begin work in their area (Council of Management minutes 1987). Three houses for people with learning disabilities and seven for those with mental health problems, many of whom had formerly lived in Storthes Hall hospital, were to be built or converted 'to enable people who have been long-stay hospital patients to enjoy a normal and better quality of life' (*St Anne's Newsletter*, December 1988) These houses eventually opened between 1989 and 1991. The significance of this expansion cannot be underestimated. Now St Anne's extended beyond Leeds; a psychological barrier had been broken after which there was little to inhibit the organisation spreading into other areas. The Council of Management decided that any such spread should only be into areas adjacent to where St Anne's was currently working for logistical, administrative and managerial reasons, however an obstacle to indefinite expansion had been breached. It is important to note that this development was achieved by invitation, admittedly an invitation extended after careful lobbying and networking. St Anne's was using the development methods that had served it so well in Leeds in areas where it was not so well known, initially with outstanding success. However no amount of solicitation and canvassing will be effective if the service does not meet the requirements of the prospective purchaser. The request that St Anne's should undertake this work was made following the successes in Leeds, and in the expectation that St Anne's would provide a top quality service at an acceptable price. St Anne's was in a near monopoly position in a new market; it had become the 'market leader' largely due to the acumen and foresight of the director and other senior managers who realised that the closure of the long-stay hospitals presented a unique opportunity to extend St Anne's provision for an increasing range of disadvantaged people.

The late 1980s saw a period of continued expansion and growth, mainly in the mental health and learning disabilities services. St Anne's was asked to play a part in the closure of Wharfe Grange Hospital, Wetherby, which required the purchase of three properties in that area and the building of a nursing home for frail, extremely dependent elderly people (Council of Management minutes 1988). The properties in Kirklees were in development, and there was a steady build-up of mental health housing in Leeds, where another hostel and three houses with visiting staff only were opened. St Anne's was continuing to investigate housing options for those leaving Shaftesbuty House. A new hostel adjacent to Head Office was built with the intention that a national agency working in substance abuse would manage it; when this funding failed to materialise St Anne's took it over as another mental health project (interview with Kilgallon, 1996) Housing for those with learning disabilities in Leeds was developing rapidly. By 1988 there were no fewer than nine such houses in Leeds – in Beeston, Headingley and Horsforth – with a further four being planned. A 'philosophy of care' guided practice in these homes. It began with the words: 'Providing ordinary housing for people with mental handicap is an attempt to break a pattern, a pattern of segregation, prejudice, deprivation and pessimism'. One of the basic tenets of this philosophy is that 'people with a mental handicap no matter what age, sex or race should be treated as members of the public and as full citizens'. (*St Anne's Newsletter*, December 1988). The move from hospital into the community was seen as a fulfilment of such a philosophy; the new staff in the new St Anne's residential services were tackling a further dimension of housing provision with the same commitment and dedication to the clients that had characterised the organisation from its creation. This achieved national recognition when Sir Roy Griffiths visited St Anne's in 1988 while researching his report.

With the Community Programme (CP) Scheme forced to finish by the end of February 1989, after much hesitation and investigation, St Anne's decided to join the new government Employment Training scheme in June 1988. A new, separate, limited company was established to train up to 250 people. Some trainees would be placed with other agencies but most would be in building or furniture workshops. Other alternatives would be added over time – for example child care, IT skills and gardening.

The whole emphasis was on training. These trainees were not initially meant to be productive for St Anne's or other agencies; in fact most had significant employment problems. St Anne's embarked on this scheme with some trepidation, aware that it would not be able to use the trainees in the same capacity as CP workers and was aware too that the ending of the CP scheme would present the organisation with a staffing crisis, especially at St Anne's Centre (interview with Costello, 1996). A new departure for St Anne's was that it was knowingly entering a competitive market. It would have to recruit trainees in competition with other trainers, and needed at least 150 per annum for the company to stay in business. A major competitor was Leeds city council, who offered £15 per week to trainees instead of St Anne's £10, and who claimed to provide superior training. St Anne's concentrated on trainees with special needs, and therefore set itself a difficult task from the beginning, as these trainees would always be the most difficult to place in jobs. The scheme was successful for several years, until changes in the funding arrangements penalised trainers of trainees with special needs, who often did not achieve impossibly high targets of output points for this client group. St Anne's Training Services Ltd, as the company had been called, was wound down in 1995, but during its seven years it had provided hope and training for many hundreds of people who would otherwise have found it considerably more difficult to access either training or employment. Its early sucesses had also enabled it to covenant its annual profits to the parent organisation, with the additional benefit of a doubling of the reserves (interview with Kilgallon, 1996).

Despite all these new activities in developing residential and training services, the original client group was not forgotten. The new premises on York Street enabled St Anne's Centre to extend and improve its services, to establish an organised volunteer scheme and to inaugurate new specialist projects for specific client groups. The day support centre in St Mark's Street was still attended mostly by people recovering from alcohol problems. Unlike York Street, it was 'dry', meaning that attenders should not have been drinking for about 24 hours before. Also, approximately half of the attenders there had permanent accommodation. A change in the profile of homelessness was becoming apparent by the mid-1980s. Both St Anne's Centre and the Detox were recording rising numbers of young people trying to access their services and the Centre particularly was seeing more women. Women had been few and far between at the original shelter, and had never been a significant problem. By the late 1980s 10 per cent of day centre attenders were female (St Anne's Centre, Survey of Attenders, 1990). Similarly, it was also unusual in the early days to see a young person; if and when one was noticed, staff quickly intervened (interviews with Kilgallon, Clair and Ryan, 1996). The problems faced by the rising numbers of young homeless people were exacerbated when the 1986 Social Security Act reduced their benefits; simultaneously organisations nationwide were becoming more alert to the problems of youngsters leaving care. In 1986, St Anne's started to consider how it could best cope with the rising tide of young people, often with multiple and complex needs, who were drifting into the Centre. It would however require a separate study to relate the experiences at St Anne's Centre to the national trends in homelessness.

Homelessness had risen throughout the 1970s with the start of cuts in the house building programme. The 1980s were characterised by a drive to home ownership and the 'right to buy', which again reduced the available stock of social housing. Repossessions peaked in 1991, obliterating many people's dreams of home ownership. Cardboard cities had sprung up in London to the extent that the government introduced its Rough Sleeper Initiative to help people off the streets. St Anne's Centre had always concerned itself with single homeless people and was only marginally affected by the major trends in the national housing market. However, as the support and resettlement advice it was able to provide became more professional and more targeted, it was able to encourage more people to move on to their own accommodation or to other more specialised agencies. The daily numbers of attenders has remained relatively constant for 25 years; but this raw data conceals the changing character and composition of the Centre's clientele and the fact that the total annual number of individuals was rising while the daily attendance figures remained more constant.

An invitation from North Yorkshire health authority similar to those from Leeds and Kirklees resulted in the acquisition of eight houses for people with learning disabilities who were leaving Whixley Hospital. These opened between 1991 and 1993 (Annual report 1993). This pattern repeated itself the following year in Calderdale, who requested a service for those leaving Stansfield View. Seven seven-bedded properties were built or converted in record time so that all the residents were rehoused by March 1993. The details of these developments mirror so closely the growth of St Anne's in Leeds and Kirklees that to detail it would be repetitious. There was further expansion in Kirklees when houses in Huddersfield and Dewsbury for people with learning disabilities transferred from the health authority to St Anne's. The opening of these houses, however, marked the end of an era. Following the 1990 Act, whereby it became a statutory duty to provide people with special needs the means to live in the community, St Anne's was no longer the lead player in a locally underpopulated marketplace. Other housing associations and even some private companies had seen a new commercial potential in residential care. Henceforth new contracts would have to be won by competitive tender, against rivals who did not necessarily place St Anne's emphasis on recruiting, retaining and training high quality staff and who could therefore undercut St Anne's costs. St Anne's now faced a harsher world and was forced to readjust its thinking.

Since 1973 St Anne's had been able to rely on statutory funding; it had of course received donations and bequests but had not gone out of its way to solicit such funds. One early recognition of the limitations of statutory funding and increased pressure for discretionary funds was the creating of a fundraising department in 1991 (Council of Management minutes 1991). Leeds city council's support for the day centre could not expand to meet the growing demands there, and gradually St Anne's was forced to find more and more of the core revenue costs. Also, to remain a needs-led organisation able to respond to the evolving needs of its clients, St Anne's was going to have to cultivate funding from charitable trusts and corporate donors to supplement its core grants. Such funding will only ever be a relatively minor proportion of St Anne's total income, but it does allow some experimental projects to be tested which, if proved successful, may be funded more securely. It also allows St Anne's to remain proactive in the development of new services where the statutory sector has neither funds nor interest. In addition, The Friends of St Anne's was established in 1992, ironically bringing the organisation back full circle to requesting funds from the community.

Between 1985 and 1993 St Anne's defined its success by its continued expansion. This changed direction in the mid-1990s, with increasing emphasis being placed on imaginative support services rather than on new buildings. Bill Kilgallon did not stand for re-election in 1992, but within months of quitting politics he had been appointed to chair the Leeds Community and Mental Health Service Teaching NHS Trust. He now shared his time between the Trust and St Anne's. Many in the organisation found difficulty in coming to terms with this, perhaps revealing an immaturity in the organisation in that it was still very dependent on one dominant leader, despite its complex management structure and well-defined procedures.

More important, with distance and the passage of time, the close networking links with the Leeds authority became less strong, as new people gradually replaced the old contacts. At the same time, Kilgallon reinforced his previous interests and contacts in the health sphere by moving as forcefully as ever into the politics of NHS Trusts, national working parties and pressure groups. His work in developing St Anne's was recognised by an OBE and many other distinctions. The old methods of networking and canvassing which had served St Anne's so well, especially in Leeds, during its formative years and its period of spectacular growth needed replacing by methods which were not centred in one charismatic and powerful persona or even a few others with long-established relationships. Faced with a dramatic increase in the number and quality of new competitors, shifts in the behaviour of existing competitors and purchasers who not only expect value for money but who are trying desperately to stem their own expenditure, St Anne's is being forced to go out into the marketplace, an activity with which it is not yet entirely comfortable.

Early forays into the competitive marketplace have not been without success. The reprovision of Castleberg Hospital, under which four new homes were opened in Craven, North Yorkshire in 1997, was an early triumph. As early as 1988 St Anne's had flagged up the possibility of increased work in Leeds and Kirklees following the proposed closure of the resettlement units, showing an awareness of trends that were still a long way into the future. It was not until 1994 that St Anne's won the tender to take over the management of the Woodhouse Project in Sheffield from the Resettlement Agency, and to bring it up to the standards of a modern hostel. This work, which included the building of 12 flats on the site, was completed in December 1997. As part of the reprovision of the resettlement unit in Leeds, St Anne's won the tender to build 34 move-on flats, which augmented the supported housing service. St Anne's had proved that it could compete. It has now to adjust to the inevitable that with these increased pressures, it is unlikely to win everything all the time. St Anne's is slowly coming to terms with the marketing demands a competitive environment necessitates.

If the developments of the mid-1990s have not be as dramatic as those of previous eras, it does not mean that they have been negligible. Holdforth Court, an award-winning resettlement hostel for homeless men, opened in 1994 to much acclaim and has provided high quality accommodation and services to over a hundred people every year. St Anne's continues to open supported housing schemes, while many smaller support schemes have been introduced – Community Carers, an adult placement scheme for people with learning disabilities; a carers support scheme to help people looking after a relative or friend with mental health problems; a research and development project to assess the needs of ethnic minorities is underway; and a befriending scheme for people with mental health problems which has been successfully established in North Kirklees. St Anne's Centre has had new kitchens and a new catering system installed, and has been refurbished. A new drop-in centre for homeless young people opened in 1996 and houses several projects, from accommodation finding and a rent bond guarantee scheme to youth and community work, open learning and drug counselling. At the same time, the needs of the more elderly homeless are catered for by a specialist project. Many of the schemes of the 1990s are support services to vulnerable groups which enhance the basic residential or day care provision established under the development and building programmes. They may not be so spectacular but they provide for a wide range of needs with flexible and adaptable support and they pressage the next phase in the development of community care, namely the progression to an independent market in domiciliary and personal services.

These support services underline the basic principle at the heart of St Anne's: that St Anne's exists to provide appropriate housing and care services to vulnerable or disadvantaged people. The success of St Anne's is not just to be measured in the visible evidence with a catalogue of new buildings and new projects – although with the scale of the operation this is difficult to avoid (Table 1.1). The organisation's success should be measured by its high-quality services, its committed and well-qualified staff, and its responsiveness to client need. The organisation has remained needs-led and its real achievements have been the improvements in the quality of life its clients now enjoy. St Anne's has weathered scandal, funding crises, the closure of some services and the rapid growth of many more. This evolution can be explained in the political, social and economic climate of the times, but St Anne's unique character has also been determined by the people who have nurtured and guided the organisation to its present strengths, especially Bill Kilgallon, the Founding Father, whose will and courage have kept the organisation true to his original vision.

Table 1.1 An overview of services at St Anne's Shelter & Housing Action

Services to homeless people

- E Day centre
- E Hostels in Leeds and Sheffield
- E Youth and community team
- E Rent bond guarantee scheme
- E Special scheme for over-55s
- E Supported housing

Alcohol services

- E Detoxification
- E Rehabilitation

Mental health services

- E Registered care homes
- E Group homes
- E Supported housing
- E Social activities
- E Befriending service
- E Carers' support service

Learning disabilities services

E Adult placement scheme

E Home support workers

E Supported housing

E Registered care homes

E Registered nursing homes

E Day centre

Supported housing

E Shared housing

E Self-contained flats

E Individual care packages

References

Allinson, P. (1985) *A Study of the Organisational Goals of a Voluntary Social Work Agency*. Dissertation, Diploma in Management Studies, Huddersfield Polytechnic.

Audit Commission (1986) *Making a Reality of Community Care*. London: HMSO.

Batley Reporter (1992) *A Calling which Led to the Night People*. 28 August 1992, p.15.

Cooper, J. (1983) *The Creation of the British Personal Social Services, 1962–74*. London:

Dant, T. and Deacon, A. (1988) *Hostels to Homes: Rehousing Homeless Single People in Leeds*. York: Joseph Rowntree Memorial Trust.

Department of the Environment (1983) *Single and Homeless*. London: HMSO.

Department of Health and Social Security (1973) *Community Services for Alcoholics*, Circular 21/73. London: HMSO.

Healy, P. (1975) *A Proposal for a Leeds Detoxification Centre* (Confidential manuscript, unpublished).

Healy, P. (1977) Aftercare Specialist Services: *A Five Yeat Phased Development Plan for the Mentally Ill among the Homeless Population in the Leeds Metropolitan District*. Confidential unpublished report.

Sandford, J. (1974) *Smiling David: The Story of David Oluwale*. London: Calder & Boyars Ltd.

Shelter (1996) *30 Years of Shelter*. London:

St Anne's Shelter & Housing Action *Annual Reports* (1972; 1973; 1979–1980; 1980–1981; 1982; 1986).

St Anne's Shelter & Housing Action *Council of Management minutes* (1982 to date).

St Anne's Shelter & Housing Action (1972) *Day Book*. (unpublished manuscript).

St Anne's Shelter & Housing Action *Newsletters* (1988; 1992 to date).

Weiler, T.G. (1971) *Habitual Drunken Offenders*. London: HMSO.

Yorkshire Evening Post (1971)

CHAPTER 2

Community Care in the Twenty-First Century

Choice, Independence and Community Integration

Gerald Wistow

Introduction

St Anne's is not the only social care agency to have celebrated 25 years of service to the community in 1996. It shares that distinction with local authority social services departments, which came into existence on 1 April 1971 with the implementation of the 1968 Seebohm Report. This joint anniversary is noteworthy for a number of reasons and not least because few, if any, observers would have predicted in the early 1970s that not-for-profit organisations would become the major providers of mainstream social care that agencies like St Anne's now are. Still less would they have anticipated social services departments themselves moving from a position of dominant supplier of residential services to that of minority provider within less than two decades. St Anne's has been both a significant contributor to, and a beneficiary of, this process of transformation in the respective responsibilities of the statutory and independent sectors. However, both the unanticipated and, until recently, largely unplanned nature of that transformation should caution against predictions about the next 25 years. Fortunately, I am required only to consider the future of community and social care into the next century, a date which, being little more than three years away, may seem sufficiently close to permit more confident speculation. However, the pace of events now seems so rapid that any predictions risk being overturned almost as soon as they are made.

For example, it is still not five years since the Health Service Commissioner (1994) issued his report on the 'Leeds case', the consequences of which have transformed the debate about the funding of community care nationally, not just in this city. Moreover, the 1997 general election raises further uncertainties about the direction of policy development and the future of social services departments. Such uncertainties particularly revolve around the Labour party's proposed royal commission on the funding of long term care and the Conservatives' promised White Paper on the personal social services.

For all these reasons, therefore, it seems even more hazardous than usual to attempt to predict the future. On the other hand, it may be observed that the existing policy base – as represented in the White Paper *Caring for People* (Secretaries of State, 1989) – is based on a clear set of values, principles and objectives which, for the most part, have attracted and continue to attract a broad consensus of support. It was also designed to initiate a long-term process of change lasting for a 'decade and beyond', as its subtitle ('Community care in the next decade and beyond') made clear. It is becoming evident that progress has been made in achieving at least some of its objectives though, as will be argued later, there are also grounds for concern about whether those goals can be more fully achieved over the longer term. Against this background, therefore, the purpose of this paper is not to provide a blueprint for community and social care over the next 25 years. Rather, it considers whether the existing policy and organisational frameworks are taking us towards the next century in directions which we fully understand or desire. Before looking to the future, however, it may be instructive to look back again to 1971 to identify some of the key elements of the environment in which St Anne's and the personal social services were born so that we can better understand the journey that has already been made as well as that for which we should now be preparing.

Perhaps the most fundamental difference between 25 years ago and today is that, in 1971, the certainties of the postwar welfare state and social contract largely remained in place. It is true that poverty had been 'rediscovered' by Abel Smith and Townsend (1966) only five years earlier, leading to an intensification of the debate about the respective merits of universal and targeted or selective benefits. Yet the basic superstructure of the welfare state remained in place and was subject to little serious challenge. Indeed, the creation of the personal social services can be seen to represent the extension and completion of that superstructure through the establishment of a 'fifth social service' (Townsend, 1971) to stand alongside the health, education, income maintenance and housing services on which the welfare state had been founded a quarter of a century previously. Hitherto the 'poor relations' of the welfare state, the personal social services were directly descended from the Poor Law, poorly funded and fragmented between local authority children's, welfare and health departments. Their unification within social services departments provided an opportunity to create comprehensive and well-resourced services, available to all, rather than the residual and predominantly institutional services of the past. However, the scale of the development task – and of the services' underfunding – was demonstrated by the fact that, until the late 1960s, spending on what became the personal social services was less than that on school meals, milk and welfare foods (Webb and Wistow, 1982).

Perhaps the most basic underpinning assumption of welfare services in 1971 was that they would be both funded and provided by the state. Charges were largely confined to residential care and met by social security payments. The state system aimed to be increasingly comprehensive in the range of needs it met and the services it provided. For the most part, it aspired to provide universal entitlements on the basis of needs rather than means and was part of the wider social contract on which the postwar welfare state was founded. Non-statutory provision was a marginal element in the service system, largely confined to relatively small scale specialist services for the 'minority' client groups, especially people with physical and learning disabilities. Public funding of the private sector was barely conceivable, the profit motive being considered incompatible with the provision of care for vulnerable people, while voluntary provision was still tarnished by association with notions of charity and stigmatisation. Indeed, the expansion of non-statutory services, if not completely an anathema outside its specialist areas, was certainly considered a retrogressive rather than a progressive step.

The state welfare model was further underwritten by national ten-year planning systems for hospital and community care services (Ministry of Health, 1962, 1963). A new system of social services planning followed the creation of social services departments and the transfer of the final elements of the health service out of local government in 1974 completed the divorce of the two systems. Indeed, an important objective of Seebohm was to establish unified social services departments as independent bases for the growth

of social work services, free from the influence of the medical profession –
and growth there certainly was: the initial ten-year plans in 1972 were based
on the assumption of 10 per cent growth per annum at compound rates and
actual spending grew by almost 20 per cent in 1972/73 and again in
1973/74. This growth target was soon scaled down but expansion continued to be rapid and spending grew by two-thirds in the first half of the
1970s compared with a fifth of public expenditure as a whole (Webb and
Wistow, 1983).

Finally, services were not only funded and planned by the state but their
delivery was dominated by the professions and other occupations it
employed. Definitions of need and the design of services reflected the views
and aspirations of the occupational groups who delivered them, with service
users cast in the role of passive recipient. For example, planning guidelines
about the volume and type of services to be provided were based on professional judgements rather than the analysis of need (Wistow, 1990) and the
notion that users might be consulted about service development would
almost certainly have seemed bizarre. For their part, service users – who were
characterised as apparently homogeneous groups of 'the elderly' or the
'mentally handicapped' – were themselves unorganised and gave due defer-
ence to the views of professionals. Carers, of course, were not even identified
as a group with their own distinctive needs.

Such then was the world into which St Anne's was born. This picture may
be overdrawn – but only slightly – and exceptions to the state welfare model
might be instanced: for example, St Anne's itself or the role of parents in
founding Mencap. However, anything other than the continuing dominance
and growth of that model was almost literally inconceivable in 1971, if only
for a few years more. Thus, the oil price rise of 1973 and the IMF funding crisis of 1976 meant that the creation of the personal social services in 1971
was in many respects the high watermark of the postwar welfare state. Since
then, the growth of public spending has been sharply reigned back (though
less severely in the personal social services than overall) and the way has been
successively opened for a wider role from: first, the voluntary sector under
the banner of 'welfare pluralism' (Webb and Wistow, 1982); second, private
providers through the introduction of social care markets; and, third, private
payments through the growth of means testing, especially for long-term
care. However, before saying more about this shift away from the state welfare model and back to a market model in the fields of social and community
care, the latter term itself requires consideration.

Although 'community care' has been talked of for more than 50 years, it has often seemed to elude precise definition and its meaning has, in any case, varied over time and in different contexts (Bayley, 1973; Walker, 1982; Webb and Wistow, 1983; Wistow, 1983). Moreover, the use of the adjective 'community' is itself problematic since it implies a greater degree of social solidarity and collective responsibility for meeting needs than has always been evident in the past or, many would argue, would be promoted by the insurance-based schemes for continuing care in which the previous Conservative government expressed some interest (Chancellor of the Exchequer and others, 1996). At the same time, the policy of community care has been criticised for being pursued on the grounds that it is cheaper than alternative forms of provision or, at best, cost neutral (House of Commons Social Services Committee, 1985). It is certainly true that the policy has been consistently characterised by a tension between the desire to contain costs and the desire to improve the quality of services (Guillebaud, 1956). There have also been tensions between different understandings of the service objectives which the policy was designed to secure. For example, an early policy document referred to the need to ensure that health and social care systems were designed 'to meet the needs of people who will wish, whether in sickness or in health, to live where ever possible in their own homes' (Ministry of Health, 1966, para 3). Other policy statements have given greater emphasis to community care as an alternative to in-patient care in both the long-stay and acute sectors, thereby extending the concept to the quaintly termed 'hospital hostels', as well as residential and nursing homes (for example DHSS, 1975). While this view underpinned NHS care *in* the community policies, social services departments have given greater emphasis to preventing unnecessary admissions *to* institutional care through the expansion of domiciliary services (Wistow, 1983). Finally, the care *by* the community policy appeared to be seeking to shift responsibilities from the state to unpaid informal carers provided by mostly female family members, friends and neighbours with formal services being relegated to the role of backstop when such care was not available (DHSS, 1981). Since the early 1980s, however, the normalisation philosophy has become an increasingly powerful influence with its emphasis on the rights of service users to be provided with individualised services in ways which respect their dignity, maximise their capacities for independent living and enable them to be integrated as fully as possible within local communities.

Major changes have taken place in the structure and organisation of services over the last quarter of a century, some of which are consistent with
community care objectives and others which are not. On the NHS side, considerable progress has been made in shifting the balance between hospital
and other forms of care. The majority of long-stay hospitals have already
closed or are planned to close in the next few years, as envisaged by the 1962
Hospital Plan (Ministry of Health, 1962). However, there remain concerns
about whether adequate levels and appropriate models of community services have been reprovided in the community. A particular issue is whether
replacement services for former long-stay patients will provide care appropriate to the needs of those who have never entered the hospitals system
(Wistow and Barnes, 1995). Substantial changes have also taken place in
acute hospital services as developments in pharmacology, medical technol-
ogy and minimal access surgery have combined with cost improvement pressures to reduce length of stay, increase day surgery rates and enable more
diagnosis, treatment and monitoring to take place outside traditional hospital settings (Wistow, 1995a; Marks, 1991). As a result, the number of acute
hospital beds fell by almost a quarter between 1982 and 1993/94, average
lengths of stay fell by more than a third, throughput increased by over 80 per
cent and day case surgery grew by more than 200 per cent (Department of
Health 1994).

A significant factor facilitating this reshaping of hospital services has
been the expansion in the number of places in residential and nursing homes.
For example, the number of long-term care places for older and younger
physically disabled people in all institutional settings more than doubled
between 1970 and 1993 (plus 106%). Within that total, the number of
long-stay hospital beds fell by a fifth, while residential home places increased
by four-fifths (81%) and nursing home places increased eightfold (803%).
Moreover, this rate of growth in institutional provision exceeded that of the
population of older people. By 1991, an estimated 27 per cent more older
people were living in long-term care institutions than would have been predicted if *per capita* levels of provision had remained constant (Laing and
Buisson, 1995). By contrast, the supply of domiciliary services failed to keep
pace with demographic growth. By 1994/95, for example, the number of
home help hours and meals had fallen by 14 per cent and 15 per cent from
their 1977/78 levels per head of population aged 75 and over (Wistow,
1996). Similar reductions took place over the next decade: between
1986/87 and 1992/93, the numbers of home helps and meals fell by 13 per

cent and 10 per cent respectively per head of population aged 75 and over (Wistow, 1996). As these data demonstrate, services developed in ways which were inconsistent with community care policy defined in terms of shifting the balance from institutional to domiciliary services: the number of residents in institutional services grew while access to domiciliary care became more difficult as services supporting people in their own homes became more thinly spread.

The growth of the independent sector

The increasing number of places provided in institutional settings was concentrated in the independent sector. Just as the volume of NHS hospital places fell between 1970 and 1993, so did the level of residential services provided by local authorities. As Table 2.1 shows, there has been a complete reversal in the respective roles of the public and independent sectors in the supply of long-stay beds. Whereas the public sector provided 69 per cent and the independent sector 31 per cent of all places in 1970, those proportions had been more than reversed by 1994 (26% and 74% respectively). Moreover, most of the growth in the independent sector took place among private rather than voluntary agencies.

Table 2.1 Long-stay beds by sector: percentage share (UK)

	Public	Private/Voluntary
1970	69	31
1988	47	53
1994	26	74

Source: Adapted from Laing and Buisson, 1995

While public-sector provision has declined rapidly, this trend has not been associated with any reduction in public-sector expenditure. Quite the reverse: much of the growth in private and voluntary homes has been funded through social security payments which were linked to institutional but not domiciliary care, and which were payable following a test of individual income/assets but not of their need for care. As a result, between 1982 and 1993 the number of residents supported by the Department of Social Security rose from 16,000 to 281,000 and the cost of supporting them rose from£39 million to£2.575 billion over the same period (House of Commons

Health Committee, 1995). With growing constraints on local authority budgets and, more importantly, with no equivalent demand-led social security
payments to finance the development of domiciliary social care services, it is
unsurprising that they failed to keep pace with the growing numbers of older
people. From the NHS perspective, the availability of social security payments directly enabled hospitals to close beds, implement early discharge
policies and shunt costs from their own budgets to the social security system.
As a result there was a significant shift in the boundary between health services free at the point of delivery and the social security system: substantial
numbers of people have moved into a means-tested system of care who might
previously have expected to receive the whole – or a much larger component
– of their care within the NHS. It is, of course, not possible to establish
beyond doubt that today's residents in nursing homes would previously have
been cared for in NHS beds, though the House of Commons Health Committee (1995, para 18) concluded that 'from our own experience of visiting
patients in nursing homes we would be surprised if this was not the case'.
What is clear is that of the 194,000 nursing home residents in 1994 (compared with only 27,000 in 1980), only 5 per cent were funded by the NHS
and thus not exposed to means testing (Table 2.2). Of the remainder, 24 per
cent were meeting their own costs and 71 per cent were funded by social
security or local authority budgets, in some cases having previously paid
their own nursing home fees until they had 'spent down' to the means-test
thresholds.

Table 2.2 Sources of funding for residents in private and voluntary nursing and residential homes for older and physically disabled people, Great Britain, February 1994

	Nursing homes		Nursing and residential homes	
	000s	Per cent	000s	Per cent
Income support	94	56	187	51
Local authorities	26	15	66	18
NHS	9	5	9	2
Self pay	41	24	102	28

Source: Adapted from Laing and Buisson, 1995

The new community care

It was against this background that the changes outlined in *Caring for People* were introduced. As the White Paper emphasised, its proposals were intended to:

E enable people to live as normal a life as possible in their own home or in a homely environment in the community

E provide the right amount of care and support to help people achieve maximum possible independence and, by acquiring or requiring basic living skills, help them achieve their full potential

E give people a greater individual say in how they live their lives and the services they need to help them do so. (Secretaries of State, 1989, para 1.11)

The White Paper further emphasised that 'promoting choice and independence underlies all the government's proposals' (*ibid.*). As will be evident, these aims owe much to the normalisation principles to which earlier reference was made. Nonetheless, there was a tension at the heart of the policy between this rhetoric about improving services and outcomes for users, on the one hand, and the less prominent (but more urgent) imperative of controlling the growth in social security spending, on the other. The competing goals of resource control and improved quality services were expected to be reconciled through the introduction of systematic needs assessment processes which would enable individuals to be diverted from residential to domiciliary care.

Implementing the new community care

Despite both the highly demanding nature of these changes and associated predictions of failure, a smooth transition to the new organisational and funding systems was achieved in 1992 and 1993 (Wistow, 1995a; Henwood, Wistow and Robinson, 1996). In addition, it has become clear that the historic pattern of investment in institutional at the expense of domiciliary services was reversed, at least initially. Thus the *per capita* level of institutional places began to fall and was only 24 per cent above its 1981 level in 1995 compared with 27 per cent in 1993 (Laing and Buisson, 1995). In addition, the number of home help contact hours increased by 41 per cent between 1992 and 1995, not least as a result of substantial growth (from 2.3% to 29%) in the independent sector's share of the local authority-funded market (Department of Health, 1996b). Not all developments since 1993 have been so positive, however. In particular, there is growing evidence that pressures on local authority resources are leading them to place limits on the costs of domiciliary care packages for which they are able and prepared to pay. Most commonly, such limits are equivalent to either the net or gross cost of a residential or nursing home placement. As a result, the Chief Social Services Inspector has acknowledged that some individuals are not being enabled to exercise their choice to remain at home (Laming, 1994). Second, there are indications that the residential and, more especially, nursing home industry is being restructured in ways that may not be compatible with the objectives of *Caring for People.*

As we have noted, that document advocated the provision of care in a 'homely environment in the local community' if people were unable to live in their own homes. Market trends are already conflicting with that objective. The average size of new homes is increasing and closures are concentrated among the smaller homes. The majority of new nursing home beds are being provided by the corporate sector which, though still a relatively small segment of the market, is growing rapidly. Small homes run by owner-managers appear to be vulnerable as market conditions favour new-build larger homes with correspondingly low unit costs. Social services departments fear that the market will become dominated by large corporate providers without local roots and providing homes with as many as 150 places (Wistow *et al.*, 1996). Thus, the preservation of the current cottage industry with its network of small, local homes is already proving difficult. These developments are not only inconsistent with policy objectives but are also heavy with irony. Local authorities took responsibility for the old Poor Law workhouses in 1948 when modern welfare services were established. Since then, they have invested considerable amounts of time and money in two activities: first, replacing those large workhouses with smaller and more modern residential units; and, second, seeking to reduce the role of residential services and enhance that of home-based care. Perhaps the ultimate implementation failure from the perspective of social services departments would be if they were compelled to buy care from new long-stay institutions as the outcome of a policy which began with efforts to close down such forms of care. Such an outcome is not inevitable but, if current trends and pressures continue, it is by no means inconceivable. The combination of financial pressures which increasingly restrict the capacity of local authorities to purchase more costly packages of care in the community, together with the pressure on unit costs in residential and nursing homes, could result in the re-emergence of new large-scale institutions rather than their final disappearance (Wistow, 1995a).

Further side effects from the introduction of the 1995 changes are the introduction of more charges and means tests. The central government grant to local authorities assumes that the latter will raise 9 per cent of their expenditure on domiciliary services through charges (an increase from 6% in the period immediately before the community care changes). As a result, many authorities have introduced charges for domiciliary services for the first time or at higher level than before (see Baldwin and Lunt, 1996). In addition, the transfer from the social security system to local government of responsibility for means tests has led to a tightening up in their administration. Whereas the social security system allowed people at least twelve months to sell their home before its value was taken into account in financial assessments, local authority rules require them to place a charge on an individual's home as soon as they enter care. One result of this change has been to raise families' awareness that they run the risk of losing their inheritance (see below). Finally, on the debit side, the community care changes have effectively underwritten the withdrawal of free health services in the long-stay sector since local authorities have been given the responsibility for purchasing nursing home care and means testing their potential residents.

Paying for continuing care

Dissatisfactions with the redrawing of the boundaries of 'free' health care and the consequential increase in means testing turned the funding of long-term care into a major political controversy. Research on public attitudes found a generalised belief that the current funding arrangements are unfair, unjust and a breach of the postwar contract (Diba, 1996). Moreover, the withdrawal of the NHS from continuing care is requiring older people to pay a second time for services they had expected to be available free at the point of delivery by virtue of their previous tax and insurance contributions. That such a major redefinition of the state's responsibility should have taken place without explicit debate undermines people's confidence in a state-led system of funding (ibid.). However, prompted by the Health Service Commissioner's report on the 'Leeds case', the government has re-emphasised that continuing care is an integral part of the NHS (Department of Health, 1995). Both the then parliamentary Under Secretary and the Chief Executive of the NHS have accepted that the service had withdrawn too far from meeting its responsibility (House of Commons Health Committee, 1995) and health authorities are being required to re-invest where they are failing to arrange and fund a full range of continuing health care services. To date, the government has refused to issue national eligibility criteria for access to such services but expects the guidance it has issued to lead to greater consistency between different parts of the country. Reliance on local eligibility criteria inevitably means that some individuals will receive free care while others with similar needs will pay for it because they live in different health authorities. However, the grosser variations seem likely to disappear and the greater explicitness about access to free health care seems likely to create pressures for the convergence of local criteria towards national norms (Wistow, 1996).

The debate about NHS responsibilities for long-term care has also led to the 'rediscovery' of the importance of rehabilitation and prevention (Department of Health, 1995). There is now an emerging acceptance that insufficient attention has been paid to the development of rehabilitation services, not least because of the previous financial incentives for the NHS to shunt costs to social security budgets for residential and nursing home care with its attendant dangers of premature institutionalisation (House of Commons Health Committee 1995, 1996). Experimental multidisciplinary and inter-agency rehabilitation schemes are now developing with initially promising results (for example, Younger-Ross, 1995). There is also growing recognition of the need to give renewed emphasis to the development of preventative strategies for healthy ageing (Lewis and Wistow, 1996). While there remains a substantial policy deficit in this area, there are the beginnings of an acceptance that the development of preventative strategies has a legitimate place in community care, not only because of the possible cost-effectiveness implications but also because they offer the prospect of a better quality of life (ADSS, Anchor Trust and DoH, 1996).

Perhaps the single most important influence shaping the debate about the future funding of long-term care has, to date, been the concern about its affordability in the context of an ageing population and doubts about the willingness and ability of informal carers to sustain existing levels of support. The tenor of this concern is exemplified by the widespread acceptance of the notion that a 'demographic time bomb' exists which will make current arrangements for state funding unsustainable and require new arrangements outside the public sector. While it is true that the numbers of people aged 85 and over who make most use of long-term care services is projected to continue growing (from 1.7% of the population in 1994 to 2.3% in 2021 and 4.8% in 2061) such figures need to be placed on context. Not only is this projected increase well below that of most other OECD (Organisation for Economic Cooperation and Development) nations, but the 400,000 projected increase in over 85-year-olds between 1994 and 2021 is actually smaller in absolute terms than the increase of 540,000 in that age group which occurred between 1971 and 1994 (House of Commons Health Committee, 1996, para 84). Moreover, the dependency ratio does not begin to worsen markedly until after 2021 (Table 2.3). Indeed, the proportion of the population aged between 15 and 64 continues to grow into the second decade of the next century. The Department of Health's analysis of a range of factors impacting upon long-term care costs concluded that its findings did 'not suggest on most reasonable assumptions that we face an impending crisis of affordability in relation to long-term care costs' (Department of Health, 1996, para 10). The House of Commons Health Committee (1996, para 116) also observed that,

> while the demand for long-term care is expected to increase in the future, projections do not support claims that we face a 'demographic time bomb' or at least not one that is likely to explode over the next two or three decades.

Demographic trends after 2031 did potentially present a greater challenge to funding but, as the same report also argued, there is 'an extended window of opportunity within which plans for dealing with this eventuality can be drawn up' (para 120). The Joseph Rowntree Foundation Report (1996) also accepted that there was no cause for immediate panic but counselled against complacency, not least because estimates of future costs become more uncertain the further they are projected into the future. Accordingly, it argued that prudence dictated that the immediate window of opportunity should be used to begin the process of building up some of the financial resources which would be needed in the future.

Table 2.3 Projected changes in the age structure in the UK population: 1994–2061

Age Group	1994	2001	2011	2021	2031	2041	2051	2061
% Aged 0 –14	19.5	19.0	17.2	16.6	16.1	15.4	15.5	15.6
% Aged 15–64	64.8	65.5	66.4	64.2	60.6	59.4	59.5	58.8
% Aged 65–84	15.0	13.6	14.3	16.9	20.4	21.4	20.1	20.8
% Aged 85+	1.7	1.9	2.1	2.3	2.9	3.8	4.9	4.8

Source: Adapted from House of Commons Health Committee, 1996

Such considerations raise questions about the mechanisms that should be used to pay for care in the next century. The Rowntree report suggested a compulsory national care insurance scheme, operating on a funded rather than a pay as you go basis and supplemented by taxation for those with insufficient contributions. The government dismissed this proposal as an 'unnecessary tax' which would impose double payments on current tax payers who would be required to pay insurance contributions for their own care whilst still meeting the care costs, through current taxation, of the current generation of older people. However, its own proposals were limited to raising the means test thresholds and publishing proposals for partnership schemes based on indemnity insurance. These proposals were vigorously criticised by the all-party Health Committee (1996), not least because the government would not provide it with estimates of their costs. It also concluded that the proposals would not provide comprehensive or universal cover and effectively constituted a state subsidy for the protection of inheritances. It might be added that, if implemented, they would represent a major policy watershed through the entry of commercial insurance into the funding of the welfare state.

Towards 2000

Over the last 25 years, the environment in which St Anne's operates has changed dramatically. There has already been a shift from a state welfare to a market model for the provision of community care. In addition, the development of policy about the funding of long-term care is now opening up a role for the market in funding as well as in providing care. A further major development has been the clarification of principles and objectives underlying community care policy (which may be summarised as the promotion of choice and independence). This framework of key objectives has been supported by attempts to remove financial incentives for the expansion of institutional rather than home care. It is now critical that the current focus on payment systems should not lose sight of the service principles underlying the policy. It sometimes appears as though the funding of long-term care is being defined in terms of establishing entitlements to residential and nursing home care based on measures of dependence rather than independence. As the Joseph Rowntree Foundation report on long-term care argued, funding mechanisms are necessary which facilitate investment in: the promotion of well being; the prevention of disease and disability; support for carers; localised and small scale residential services; and domiciliary health and social care services (Joseph Rowntree Foundation, 1996).

Second, choice and independence are insufficient in themselves as underlying principles for community care policy in the next century. They can be interpreted in a narrowly individualistic way and say nothing about social inclusion and social solidarity. Indeed, they may come to be associated more with the management of dependence than the promotion of independence. Complex packages of personal care may enable more people to live in their own homes, but if they have few social contacts and little engagement with the communities in which they live, the quality of life provided is of questionable value. Moreover, as Fletcher has argued, increased targeting on a small number of individuals with relatively high support needs leads to a focus on the individual rather than the community in which they live. A preventative approach also implies an emphasis on the community and especially as a focus for involvement in activities which promote engagement and a sense of well being and personal worth (Fletcher, 1996). The Anchor local service network model provides an example of this approach. The intention is to develop partnerships between statutory agencies, independent sector providers, community groups and older people to ensure good local information services; active community centres and social clubs; community involvement in caring and support; and service development built around what service users identify as being important to them. It provides what is, in effect, an example of the community development approach to social care which the Seebohm report advocated but which has never been fully adopted.

Third, the more we emphasise the role of the community in community care, the more it follows that housing is not only the foundation of community care but the key to its successful implementation. Community care is, by definition, a housing agenda: independent living in the community for people resettled from long-stay hospitals depends upon the supply of good quality accommodation adapted to their needs just as much as the provision of personal care and support. Similarly, housing conditions and environments are key factors in whether individuals are able to remain in their own homes rather than enter institutional care. The value of 'staying put' and 'care and repair' services are now well documented in this respect and the research also suggests that they are particularly beneficial if provided on a preventative basis rather than as a response to crisis when people have begun to become frail (Lewis and Wistow, 1996). The lifetime homes concept being supported by the Rowntree Foundation is a similarly important development. The contribution of housing is not, however, merely to provide the accommodation within which people live: it is also an expression of values which support independent living – tenants and owner-occupiers have rights over their own lives which residents do not so easily share. Potentially, therefore, housing services can reinforce notions of choice and independence which professional care services may find more difficult if not threatening.

Finally, social inclusion has been referred to in terms of engagement within the community. However, the social contract is another important dimension of social inclusion. There is no doubt that the unannounced, if not surreptitious, way in which entitlements to free health care were defined away during the 1980s has been seen as a betrayal of trust and obligations which formed part of the cement for the welfare state and our sense of community. The miss-selling of personal pensions and endowment policies has similarly damaged confidence in the market. Thus, we are approaching the year 2000 with justified public feelings that neither the state nor the market can be fully trusted to provide secure funding for care on the terms the post-war generation had reason to expect. Whatever the respective roles of the state and the market in the next century, there is a clear need for a new social contract which is regulated effectively so that it is less vulnerable to market failures or to policy making by stealth.

References

Abel Smith, B. and Townsend, R. (1966) *The Poor and Poorest.* Occasional Papers in Social Administration, No.17. London: G. Bell and Sons.

ADSS, Anchor Trust and Department of Health (1996) *Preventative Services for Older People and Community Care: Findings from a Joint Policy Seminar* held on 17 September 1996. Oxford: Anchor Trust.

Baldwin, S. and Lunt, N. (1996) *Charging Ahead.* Bristol: Policy Press.

Bayley, M. (1973) *Mental Handicap and Community Care: A Study of Mentally Handicapped People in Sheffield.* London: Routledge and Kegan Paul.

Chancellor of the Exchequer, Secretary of State for Social Security, President of the Board of Trade, Secretary of State for Health, Secretary of State for Northern Ireland, Secretary of State for Scotland and Secretary of State for Wales (1996) *A New Partnership for Care in Old Age: A Consultation Paper,* CM 3242. London: HMSO.

Department of Health and Social Security (1981) *Care in Action.* London: HMSO.

Department of Health and Social Security (1975) *Better Services for the Mentally Ill,* Cmnd6233. London: HMSO.

Department of Health (1994) *NHS Hospital Activity Statistics: England 1983–1994,* Statistical Bulletin. London: Department of Health.

Department of Health (1995) *NHS Responsibilities for Meeting Continuing Health Care Needs,* HSG (95) 8/LAC (95) 5. London: Department of Health.

Department of Health (1996a) 'Projecting future public expenditure on long-term care: supplementary memorandum submitted by the Department of Health.' In House of Commons Health Committee, *Long-Term Care: Future Provision and Funding,* Session 1995–96, Third Report, Vol. 2, Minutes of Evidence and Appendices, HC59-II. London: HMSO.

Department of Health (1996b) *Community Care Statistics 1995,* Statistical Bulletin. London: Department of Health.

Diba, R. (1996) *Meeting the Costs of Continuing Care.* York: Joseph Rowntree Foundation.

Fletcher, P. (1996) 'The relationship between housing and community care.' *Journal of Interprofessional Care 10,* 3, 249–56.

Guillebaud, C.W. (1956) *Report of the Royal Commission on the Cost of the NHS,* CMD9663. London: HMSO.

Health Service Commissioner (1994) *Failure to Provide Long-Term NHS Care for a Brain-Damaged Patient,* second report for session 1993–4, HC197. London: HMSO.

Henwood, M., Wistow, G. and Robinson, J. (1996) 'Halfway there? Policy, politics and outcomes in community care.' *Social Policy and Administration 30,* 1, 1–19.

House of Commons Health Committee (1995) *Long-Term Care: NHS Responsibilities for Meeting Continuing Health Care Needs,* first report for session 1995–96, HC19-I. London: HMSO.

House of Commons Health Committee (1996) *Long-Term Care: Future Provision and Funding*, third report for session 1995–96, HC59-I. London: HMSO.

House of Commons Social Services Committee (1985) *Community Care*, second report for session 1984–85, HC13. London: HMSO.

Joseph Rowntree Foundation Enquiry (1996) *Meeting the Costs of Continuing Care*. York: Joseph Rowntree Foundation.

Laing and Buisson (1995) *Care of Elderly People: Market Survey 1995*, eighth edition. London: Laing and Buisson Publications.

Laming, H. (1994) *Putting People First*. The third annual report of the Chief Inspector, Social Services Inspectorate, 1993–94. London: HMSO.

Lewis, H. and Wistow, G. (1996) *Preventative Services for Older People: Current Approaches and Future Opportunities*. Oxford: Anchor Trust.

Marks, L. (1991) *Home and Hospital Care: Re-Drawing the Boundaries*, Research Report No. 9. London, King's Fund.

Ministry of Health (1962) *A Hospital Plan for England and Wales*, Cmnd1604. London: HMSO.

Ministry of Health (1963) *The Development of Community Care*, Cmnd 1973. London: HMSO.

Ministry of Health (1966) *The Hospital Building Programme: A Revision of the Hospital Plan for England and Wales*, Cmnd3000. London: HMSO.

Secretaries of State (1989) *Caring for People: Community Care in the Next Decade and Beyond*, CM849. London: HMSO.

Seebohm Report (1968) *Report of the Committee on Local Authority and Allied Personal Services*, Cmnd 3703. London: HMSO.

Townsend, P. (1971) *The Fifth Social Service*. London: Fabian Society.

Walker, A. (1982) 'The meaning and social division of community care.' In A. Walker (ed) *Community Care: The Family, The State and Social Policy*. Oxford: Basil Blackwell and Martin Robertson.

Webb, A. and Wistow, G. (1982) *Whither State Welfare? Policy Implementation in the Personal Social Services 1979–80*. London: Royal Institute of Public Administration.

Webb, A. and Wistow, G. (1983) 'Public expenditure and policy implementation: the case of community care.' *Public Administration 61*, 1, 21–44.

Wistow, G. and Barnes, M. (1995) 'Central Nottinghamshire, England: A Case Study of Managed Innovation in Mental Health.' In R. Schulz and J. Greenley (eds) *Innovating in Community Mental Health: International Perspectives*. Westport, USA: Greenwood Publishing Group.

Wistow, G. (1983) 'Joint finance and community care: have the incentives worked?' *Public Money 3*, 2, 33–7.

Wistow, G. (1990) *Community Care Planning: A Review of Past Experience and Future Imperatives*. Caring for People Implementation Document CCI3. London: Department of Health.

Wistow, G. (1995a) 'Aspirations and realities: community care at the crossroads.' *Health and Social Care in the Community 3*, 4, 227–240.

Wistow, G. (1995b) 'Long term care: who is responsible?' In A. Harrison (ed) *Health Care UK 1994/95*. London: King's Fund Policy Institute.

Wistow, G. (1996) 'The changing scene in Britain.' In T. Harding, B. Meredith and G. Wistow (eds) *Options for Long Term Care*. London: HMSO.

Wistow, G., Knapp, M., Hardy, B., Forder, J., Kendall, J. and Manning, R. (1996) *Social Care Markets: Progress and Prospects*. Buckingham: Open University Press.

Younger-Ross, S. (1995) *Outlands: A Community Care Support Centre*. Exeter: Social Services Department, Devon County Council.

CHAPTER 3

Changing Values in the Field of Mental Health

Alan Butler

Introduction

St Anne's was born in 1971, not by coincidence, at a time of great optimism in the field of mental health.

As Wistow notes elsewhere in this book, local authority social service departments came into being on All Fools Day that year. This followed the Seebohm Report published some three years earlier (1968). The Seebohm Committee, established in 1965, was charged with the task of 'reviewing the organisation and responsibilities of the local authority personal social services in England and Wales and to consider what changes are desirable to secure an effective family service.' (Seebohm Report, 1968, p.1).

The eventual creation of a single body responsible for social welfare within each local authority – the social services department – reflected, among other issues, a concern for the lack of coordination between previously existing welfare organisations, and the quickening interest in community care policies. An unintended consequence was the creation of a monolithic, bureaucratic organisation with virtual monopoly powers in a large geographical area.

The transformation of St Anne's began, in part, as a reaction to this state of affairs. Innovative services, customised and designed to meet individual needs to high standards, became easier to generate without the weight of local authority officialdom.

The consolidation of welfare was accompanied by the continuing desire to run down the large psychiatric hospitals. Mental health beds have fallen by 75 per cent in the past 40 years, with about 50,000 disappearing since 1980.

Sir Keith Joseph, Minister of Health and longstanding Leeds MP, argued in an important 1971 memorandum (*Hospital Services for the Mentally Ill*, DHSS, 1971) that the number of beds should continue to fall. However, he detected two problems that have continued to dog us, and to which St Anne's has responded. The first was the accumulation of what, at the time, were identified as the 'new long-stay' patients. The realisation that the run-down and eventual closure of the large asylums was not simply a case of finding alternatives for the existing population – difficult as that has proved – but that there were newly developing cases, usually people suffering from schizophrenia, for whom medium-term hospital care was inevitable in the absence of realistic alternative accommodation.

Second, there was an absence of mandatory powers within mental health legislation. The new Seebohm departments had certain statutory powers, but the provision of accommodation and day care for the mentally ill or those suffering learning disabilities were not among them. This meant that some local authorities failed to provide sufficient services for these groups. This led to uneven provision across the country and some alarming gaps that organisations such as St Anne's began to explore. By the time Barbara Castle assumed the role of Secretary of State for Social Services and issued the White Paper *Better Services for the Mentally Ill* (DHSS, 1975) it was noted that '31 local authorities, as then constituted, had no residential accommodation for the mentally ill, and 63 no day facilities' (DHSS, 1975, p.ii).

Over the following 25 years there have been a number of important changes that have impacted upon the provision and delivery of mental health services: a new Mental Health Act; the Griffiths Report, and the development of the 'mixed economy of welfare', among others.

However, as a way of charting some of the influences and changes upon St Anne's, and its way of working, I have chosen to focus upon their mission statement 'Values and Beliefs'. This document neatly encapsulates many of the changing values to be found in the mental health field in the past 25 years. In order to conduct this archeology of ideas and shifting beliefs and values, I have chosen to focus upon four broad areas:

E medication

E housing

E normalisation

E quality of life.

Medication

The statement about medication is a very interesting one, reflecting as it does a major shift in professional and lay opinion in a period of years, and it is worth repeating in full:

> Many people living in our accommodation are prescribed medication to control or alleviate symptoms of mental illness. Medication provides benefits but also negative side effects, both physical, psychological and social. We see our role as encouraging users to cooperate with medical regimes but that we should work with users and others to ensure that medication is kept at a minimum level; we would normally encourage people to continue with medication, particularly if their past experience suggests that their health may deteriorate without this. However we will, if they so wish, actively support them in seeking to lower the level of medication as much as possible.

The introduction of psychotropic drugs, such as chlorpromazine and reserpine, in the 1950s is thought by many to have triggered a period of therapeutic optimism and a consequent shift towards early hospital discharge and declining bed numbers (Butler and Pritchard, 1983). The enthusiasm may, however, have led to both overuse and overvaluation of their impact.

As Warner noted (1985):

> The antipsychotic drugs have emerged as a routine, almost automatic, remedy in psychosis and relatively little effort has been made in psychiatry to use these medicines selectively. One might search a long time to find a diagnosed schizophrenic who has never been treated with a neuroleptic. It may be better, however, to avoid the use of antipsychotic drugs in the case of substantial numbers of these patients, but the existence of such subgroups of schizophrenics has not been well recognised (p.239).

Andrew Scull, among others, in his book *Decarceration* (1977) also began to question the easy assumption that more use of drugs led inevitably to greater levels of hospital discharge. He, like Warner, noted that this logic was defective in terms of timing. The decline in psychiatric beds, both here and in the USA, was detectable before chlorpromazine (largactic/thorazine) was widely available in about 1954. The realisation began to spread that whilst the new medications may help to control or contain some of the symptomatology, they did not offer the hope of permanent cure. Scull indeed claimed that 'A growing volume of evidence … suggests that claims about the therapeutic effectiveness of so-called "anti-psychotic" medication … have been greatly exaggerated' (pp.79–82).

A major concern about widespread and heavy medication of mental health sufferers was the potential side effects. Some were proving dangerous in overdose and became the favoured method for suicide. The neuroleptic drugs were creating unfortunate neurological side effects such as tardive dyskinesia – involuntary and embarrassing movements of the jaws, tongue and other parts of the body, together with difficulties with speech and swallowing. Warner (1985) noted that as many as one-third of outpatients taking antipsychotic drugs were exhibiting these disturbing symptoms.

The belief that medication would provide an easy solution to our mental health problems began to be tempered by this fresh evidence about its potentially damaging effects. Various user groups began to campaign around the issues and alert professionals to their concerns.

Kleinman, Schacter and Koritar (1989) in the USA highlighted the high risks involved and the potential irreversibility of tardive dyskinesia. They called attention to the meaning and importance of the term 'informed consent':

> To be adequately informed, a patient must understand the nature, benefits and risks of the proposed treatment as well as the benefits and risks of the alternative choices, including no treatment (p.904).

The authors noted how infrequently patients were being informed about the risks: only 32 per cent of psychiatrists did this as a matter of routine.

British practice may, in part, be driven by shortages of personnel and lack of resources. Paradoxically, it could be easier to heavily medicate an individual living in the community and risk side effects, rather than proffer a more expensive system of regular monitoring and lower doses. McClelland (1989) for example, cited in Barham (1992), acknowledged that:

> The present stereotyped drug regime administered to all patients cannot be the best clinical practice … many patients … do very well on smaller amounts than what are usually regarded as 'standard' doses (p.127).

Without the ability to monitor those taking these powerful medicines closely the pressure to come up with cost-effective solutions may lead to patients with 'greasy, masked faces, stooped posture, dancing feet and shuffling gait'

(Jolley, Hirsch and Manchanda, 1989, p.990) – a situation that the consumers may judge as being worse than the original illness.

The philosophy adopted by St Anne's reflects the idea that the recipients have the right to their own views about their medication. Kleinman *et al.* (1989) note that for consent to be meaningful it must be 'viewed as an educational process and not as a single isolated event marked by the signing of a consent form' (p.904). Moreover the challenge, as they see it, 'is to effectively treat these patients while respecting their individuality and their autonomy. Informing patients about their illness and the positive and negative aspects of treatment is the first step in an educational process that may span years.'

As Newton (1992) concludes in her important book that attempts to develop preventive strategies in the mental health field:

> The work on early warning signs, linked with targeted use of neuroleptic medication, is promising to have exciting implications for long term sufferers of schizophrenia. Such close monitoring of symptoms will make it easier for treatment services to set maintenance doses at the lowest possible level, but may also, in a small proportion of cases, mean that maintenance medication may be discontinued and replaced by intermittent targeted usage of the drugs. Research is continuing on this approach, but it will probably be most appropriate in the context of a family education and support programme. (p.163)

Housing

Gerald Wistow, elsewhere in this volume, notes that

> Community care is, by definition, a housing agenda: independent living in the community for people resettled from long-stay hospitals depends upon the supply of good quality accommodation adapted to their needs, just as much as personal care and support. Similarly, housing conditions and environments are key factors in whether individuals are able to remain in their own homes rather than enter institutional care.

The last point was made forcefully by Peter Townsend back in 1962 in his book on the institutionalising of older people, *The Last Refuge*, and yet it is just as relevant today.

A core belief for St Anne's is that: 'the need for a home is fundamental for most people and without this it is extremely difficult for any individual to build a satisfactory way of life.' Since 1971, successive governments have sought to encourage owner-occupation and restrict public expenditure on housing. Housing, along with defence, is one of the few areas of government expenditure to have fallen, in real terms, over the past 25 years. The results have been plain for us all to see:

E mortgage failure

E negative equity

E poor levels of maintenance

E gross shortages of housing to rent

E large rent rises in the public sector

E high levels of homelessness.

The policies have also tended to concentrate the poorest and most vulnerable of our citizens into neighbourhoods of intense deprivation, high levels of vandalism and social problems such as alcoholism and other addictions (Power and Tunstall, 1995).

Leigh (1994), in a recent report on community care and the single homeless, identified the failure of central government to fund the system adequately, particularly with regard to those with mental health problems:

> The current range of affordable housing options for people with mental health problems has been limited by government housing policies and by a lack of imagination at a local level about alternatives to hospital admission (like sanctuary houses). (p.1)

The Nuffield Provincial Hospitals Trust, in a report (1994), makes a similar point when it highlights the lack of affordable and adequate housing and warns of the negative consequences this has for both physical and mental health problems.

The impact of poor or inadequate housing upon mental health has been commented upon by Hyndman (1990), who noted increased levels of depression and anxiety, and Hunt (1990), who linked overcrowding to psychological distress.

As Rogers and Pilgrim (1996) comment, this raises important issues about the right to good accommodation – something acknowledged by the St Anne's 'Values and Beliefs' statement:

> A separate issue is that of accommodation rights in a post-institutional world. The old asylums were warehouses for madness. Acute psychiatric units cannot serve the same function although, in practice the speed of discharge of patients can be currently influenced by the lack of availability of appropriate accommodation. Consequently, hospitalisation is a solution for neither homelessness nor inadequate housing

for people with mental health problems. (Rogers and Pilgrim 1996, p.198)

Range of options

A wide range of housing options, with or without support, is now possible. However, as I comment elsewhere, availability in a given geographical area may be severely restricted. My own work (Butler, Oldman and Greve, 1983) has tended to concentrate upon sheltered housing, most readily associated with older people. A number of schemes have included or been dedicated to both younger disabled people and those suffering mental health problems. The term 'sheltered housing' in reality itself covers a wide range of schemes and a variety of tenure arrangements (buy, rent or own).

A government circular in the late 1960s established two broad types of scheme:

E Category 1 consists of purpose-built flats or bungalows with a warden, but often with no common room or other facilities for shared use.

E Category 2 is usually identified as a scheme with individual bungalows or flats linked by heated internal corridors. A common room, laundry and guest room, and other facilities for shared use, are normally included. (Ministry of Housing and Local Government, 1969)

With increasing dependency levels among tenants some people have talked about Category 2½ schemes whereby extra domiciliary and welfare support is dedicated to the housing complex.

Bayliss (1987), in a major review of the relationship between housing and community care, outlined the following other possibilities in the mental health field:

1.   Fully self-contained flats with bedroom, living room, kitchen and bathroom and WC.

2.   Self-contained bedsitters, usually a combined bedroom/living room with a separate kitchen and bathroom/WC, although some bedsitters also have the kitchen in the main room.

3.   Shared housing, which can encompass a variety of arrangements, including: own bedsitter and shared kitchen and bathroom; own bedroom and shared living/dining room, kitchen and bathroom.

Some meals may be eaten communally, for example in the evenings and/or at weekends.

4. Cluster flats: self-contained flats or bedsitters in a single house. Tenants cater for themselves and essentially live independently, but may share some facilities such as a laundry room. Individual cluster flats may be for one or more people.

5. Staffed hostels, which may be short-stay or cater for people on a more permanent basis; they may have shared or single bedrooms. The level of staff support can vary considerably.

6. Shared living schemes, where people with learning disabilities or mental health problems share a house with 'able tenants' who offer varying degrees of support. Many of these schemes have been developed in university towns, with students as 'able tenants'.

7. Residential care homes, registered under the 1984 Residential Homes Act, often similar in accommodation and style to staffed hostels, but with a greater range of services provided, such as meals.

8. Crisis or 'asylum' housing which can be used on a short or medium-term basis by people undergoing a crisis.

Hostel provision

In 1971 the hostel was considered to be one of the most appropriate forms of accommodation for someone suffering a long-term mental health problem, particularly those being discharged from hospital. The problem we have discovered, in the intervening 25 years, is that there is a severe danger that they may become just as institutional as the former long-stay ward. The quality of life offered to many hostel dwellers seems just as impoverished as that offered to somebody in a former asylum.

Barham and Hayward (1995) have undertaken some important ethnographic work among formerly hospitalised psychiatric patients. Ben, for example, comments that 'I was put into a hostel. I was homeless and so I had to go somewhere'(p.37). Another respondent notes that the hostel '... would have been all right if it had acted as a community but everybody was very isolated and although we might go for a drink with somebody from time to time we didn't function as a house – it was individuals living close together but isolated' (Barham and Hayward, 1995, p.40).

Adequate housing is not just about the physical aspects of a building – dampness, heating, and so on – it also is about some of the other things I mention in this chapter, such as autonomy and choice.

Sarah, for example, moved from a hostel to a small flat offering both privacy and a sense of a space being her own: 'I'm more able to invite people back without having the problems of explaining why I'm living here' (Barham and Hayward, 1995, p.42).

Much of the work Barham and Hayward did was conducted in Bradford. A little earlier, in York, another city close to Leeds, Kathleen Jones and colleagues were interviewing ex-psychiatric patients. She concluded (Jones, 1988) that 'Patients who had gone into hostels had not materially changed their quality of life. Hostels tended to be somewhat spartan, the food and living conditions no better than those in hospital' (p.126).

She noted that her respondents had a 'marginally greater degree of freedom of movement ... but ... no more privacy' (p.126), and summed up the experience of moving from hospital to the community for many ex-patients by saying that 'the move had the effect of taking patients off the hospitals' books, but made comparatively little difference in terms of daily living'.

A consistent finding throughout the past 25 years has been that accommodation for mental health sufferers is very unevenly distributed across the country. As long ago as 1975 the White Paper *Better Services for the Mentally Ill* noted that:

> Although it is 16 years since the Mental Health Act of 1959 gave legislative recognition to the importance of community care, supportive facilities in a non-medical, non-hospital setting are still a comparative rarity. In 1973–74 nearly £300 million was spent on hospital services for the mentally ill; by comparison just over £15 million was spent on personal social services, of which some £6.5 million was on day and residential facilities. In March 1974, 31 local authorities, as then constituted, had no residential accommodation for the mentally ill, and 63 no day facilities. (DHSS, 1975, p.iii)

The work of Watson and Cooper (1992) more recently was just as critical of the lack of coherent revenue support systems for high care housing schemes. They also point to the importance of good coordination between social service departments, now the lead agency in community care, and housing associations. To this could be added the problematic interface between social services and health, a subject which is attracting increasing governmental attention. The differences of culture between key agencies was something that I identified in my work on sheltered housing (Butler *et al.* 1983). Similar signs of friction have been evident, at times, within St Anne's itself. On occasions, the housing arm of the organisation – intent upon keeping accommodation filled – has bumped uneasily against those from a social work background, their focus of interest being the individual needs of a particular user.

In evidence to the 1982 Barclay Committee, which was looking at the future for social work, the Institute of Housing submitted the following statement:

> Unfortunately, in many cases the working relationships between housing officers and social workers are not good ... generally speaking they view each other with considerable scepticism. There is a stereotyped image of the social worker as young and freshly qualified, straight from school via college, without any practical experience, who would be entirely subjective and idealistic about clients and will seek all manner of handouts and special treatment for them, without ever expecting them to stand on their own feet. By contrast, the housing officer might see himself as objective and fair in ordering priorities for the allocation of houses. He would probably employ ... techniques of management which he believes will develop independence and self-respect for the common good. The Institute of Housing sub-committee is of the opinion that these prejudices all too often turn out to be true. (Quoted in Means and Smith, 1994, p.190)

There are dangers inherent in focusing upon 'special needs housing' as I (Butler *et al.*, 1983) and others (Means, 1987; Wheeler, 1988) have noted. The argument being that central government concentration upon the need for specialised schemes deflects attention away from the need to provide appropriate and affordable mainstream provision.

More recently, Clapham and Smith (1990) pointed out that

> 'special needs' is a selective redefinition of housing disadvantage, which portrays housing problems as discrete and technical (and therefore politically manageable) and provides criteria for discriminating between groups who are more or less deserving of a share in the progressively limited pool of public funds. (p.204)

Users and empowerment

One of the ways in which we may appreciate changing social values is by examining the words that we use to describe people. In 1971 those using

medical or psychiatric services were patients; those receiving the ministra-
tions of social workers, clients.

In the following 25 years, various terms have been advanced as substitutes
for patient/client. This has been part of a conscious attempt to reduce the
apparent power of the professional and enhance that of the 'user' – the term
St Anne's currently adopts. The user's voice is now much clearer and more
sharply defined in the planning and delivery of services.

As Barham comments:

> One way in which to describe the promise that is held out by the shift
> from the mental patient (person) to the person (mental patient) is of
> deliverance from a tradition of welfare paternalism in which the
> beneficiaries were the passive recipients of care and the voice of the
> mentally ill was all but silenced (Barham, 1992, p.112).

Barham's (1992) intensive interviewing with those suffering from a mental
illness in the community led him to agree that the experience of the mentally
ill was 'one of disempowerment, loss of control over their lives, a sense of
being at the receiving end of being a passive recipient' .(MIND 1989, p.13)

Throughout the 1980s the free market was lauded as the beneficent
invisible hand that would empower us all. The market, it was believed, was
the best system available to allocate resources and deal with economic
shortages and rationing. Patients and clients became 'consumers' for a brief
period of time as they were encouraged to regard community care as a great
market hall in which they were free to shop. MIND, for example,
championed the term for a while and developed its 'consumer network'. The
high point of this period was reached possibly when supermarket supremo
Sir Roy Griffiths was charged, by government, with the task of examining
the future delivery of community care.

As a way of recognising the damage that institutional psychiatry had
done, or was doing, to some people, the term 'survivor' was adopted by certain groups for a period of time (Lawson, 1991). Hence the emergence of
organisations such as 'Survivors Speak'. Similar groups also championed the
term 'recipient', once again seeking to emphasise their apparent powerless-
ness in the face of psychiatric establishment.

The term 'user' holds current sway, the attraction being its apparent neu-
trality. However, its association with illegal drug use in the public's mind may
limit its currency.

Underpinning this toying with language are concerns about the stigma-
tising impact of certain words and the desire to empower users and adopt

policies which are associated with the concept of normalisation. These are clearly reflected in the 'seven accomplishments' identified by John O'Brien in the St Anne's policy statement.

The concept of normalisation, or 'social valorisation' as it is now termed, developed in the early 1970s in North America. Wolfensberger and colleagues (1973, 1983) sought to establish the rights of mentally disabled people, many of whom had been discharged from large hospitals in order to live in the community. In the past, they reasoned, rehabilitation and adjustment to life outside had been undermined by the low social value and esteem attributed to them by members of the wider society. In order to challenge and confront the attitudes, Wolfensberger and colleagues urged that two goals should be established. The first should be the enhancement of the individual's social image. Practically, this meant that the accommodation that they occupied should be physically attractive and similar to that lived in by the rest of the population. Occupation and leisure activities should also be similar to that of the local populace; the ambition being that the newcomers would integrate into the local community. Second, service providers should aim to 'enhance the competency' of users, thus ensuring that they could make wide use of local rather than specialist services. Within St Anne's these ideas have powerfully shaped the ways in which service and accommodation is conceptualised and delivered. The extent to which users now visit local amenities such as pubs and bowling alleys and go on holiday together is well illustrated by the various user-led newsletters that the organisation supports.

Normalisation theorists have drawn attention to the fact that a disability does not reside solely in the designated individual. It is a deficit created by the interaction between that individual and the wider society and the environment it offers. The plight of many mental health sufferers has been exacerbated by their exclusion from the mainstream and their exposure to poor-quality services and impoverished institutional regimes. As a consequence, normalisation theory gave intellectual support and nourishment to the growth of advocacy work and the increasing emphasis being placed, in recent years, upon individual rights.

Barker and Peck (1988) indicate that advocacy work, in the field of mental health, is concerned with strengthening the voice of service users in determining the provision of services. In their review they identify two broad types; those schemes that are concerned with group issues and activities and those that focus upon issues of individual care.

The establishment of a local Mental Health Forum, with members drawn from current and former mental health service users, is typical of a group activity. They act, sometimes with professional support or help, as lobbyists to improve standards locally or highlight deficiencies in services.

Individual advocacy models also fall into two broad categories. Self-advocacy encourages people to represent their own views, and may involve some form of training or coaching by a specialist body. For those who might find this too difficult to accomplish, schemes exist whereby trained volunteers or professional workers may act as advocates on their behalf.

Within the St Anne's documentation various acknowledgements are made of the need to empower users, facilitate choice and encourage self-advocacy. The provision of a key worker, for example, may help to fulfil the advocacy function, whilst the announcement that 'We will encourage residents to express views and opinions and to organise themselves so as to formulate and express their views with regard to our service provision' is clearly an attempt to foster 'group advocacy'.

Quality of life

One of the major changes over the past 25 years in the field of mental health, has been the emergence of the concept 'quality of life'. Implicit acknowledgement of this is to be found in the listing of human needs in the policy statement:

E physical care

E housing

E health care

E social and sexual relations

E education and training

E jobs and positions of responsibility

E spiritual fulfilment.

All of which, the document asserts, the St Anne's clientele are entitled to expect 'to a good standard'.

In 1971 the focus for mental health professionals was much more likely to involve a discussion about the importance of differential diagnosis and the measurement of outcome by means of clinical criteria – changes in symptomatology, remission and so on (Butler and Pritchard, 1983).

Today, far greater attention is paid, in the case of those suffering long-term mental health problems, to the quality of life that they are enabled to lead. In part, this reflects a changing emphasis in the wider world of social research where quantitative methodologies are now being challenged by those adopting a qualitative approach to measurement.

In 1985 the ESRU held a conference in Edinburgh under the title *Planning to Care – Social Policy and the Quality of Life*. Robertson and Osborn (1985), in the resultant monograph, noted that:

> Resonating as it does with a human sense that our experience of living can be comprehended and evaluated as a coherent whole, the term 'quality of life' has obvious attractions for the planners, managers and providers of social services. It implies a framework within which the activities of the various services may be related to a set of overall objectives. (p.1)

Noting the shift from quantitative to qualitative research, Sinfield (Robertson and Osborn, 1985) noted that: 'Knowledge of people was almost entirely a matter of body counts' (p.9).

An added boost was given to the interest in quality of life by the increasing attempts being made by economists to measure and cost various forms of health and welfare provision. As Baldwin, Godrey and Propper (1990) note:

> Economic analysis of markets in which prices are absent, such as the health and social services markets, has brought to the fore the question of appropriate measures of output and outcome. To evaluate interventions in the field of acute health care, economists have begun to develop quality of life measures. While not necessarily an output measure, change in the quality of patients' lives is clearly one outcome of an intervention in the market. (p.1)

Asserting the importance of quality of life is one thing, trying to capture it and then apply some form of measurement is quite another. The starting point for most attempts is the work of Abraham Maslow (1971) and his concept of the 'hierarchy of human needs'. He identified five domains of need and suggested that one must be satisfied before the individual could fully experience the next.

Domains of need

1. Survival – food, drink, sleep, shelter from the elements.
2. Stability – avoidance of uncertainty and possible danger.

3. Purpose – work, meaningful leisure, companionship.

4. Autonomy – a degree of independence, personal space and privacy.

5. Aesthetic and intellectual satisfaction. (Based on Maslow)

Early attempts to operationalise the concept for evaluative purposes tended to group together existing tools into a large bundle. Emotional well-being was adjudged by means of life-satisfaction or self-esteem measures. Psychological well-being was usually reduced to an off-the-shelf measure of anxiety and/or depression. Social well-being utilised indicators of social network or community integration. Finally, the physical well-being dimension was encapsulated by measures of physical health status or functioning.

The process was refined when Lehman, Ward and Lynn (1982) and Lehman (1988); Lehman in the USA developed a structured interview schedule to be used with individuals suffering chronic mental health problems. The conceptual model is based upon an attempt to capture a global picture of well-being by focusing upon the life circumstances of the individual in terms of what they actually do and experience (objective factors) and their feelings about these experiences (subjective factors).

Initially, eight life domains were identified:

E family relations

E social relations

E work

E finances

E safety

E health

E leisure

E living situation.

To these were later added religion, and in some versions a measure of neighbourhood, something that I was also trying to develop, along with Joe Oliver, at about the same time (Oliver and Butler, 1979).

This model proved to be the launching pad for significant developments in this country. In the early 1990s Joe Oliver and his colleagues in Manchester (Oliver et al., 1995) developed the Lancashire quality of life profile which has since been used widely in both this country, Europe and North America.

The Lancashire quality of life profile uses both subjective and objective measures in order to review a variety of domains. It has been subject to a number of validity and reliability checks and is now being used as a routine instrument in various parts of Lancashire in order to assess people's well-being. It also may be used to indicate which remain in deficit, hence providing a focus for practical interventions and support.

Results from major quality of life studies – particularly those conducted by Oliver and colleagues in Lancashire (Oliver *et al.*, 1995) – demonstrate that community treatment is more popular with users and that both mental health and the network of social relationships can be improved. However, such studies also highlight the major deficiencies in current provision, in particular the lack of meaningful work or occupation during the day (something the former institutions were able to provide in plenty); unacceptable levels of poverty and the unevenness in quality of accommodation. Huxley (1996), developing the Lancashire data, indicates that quite high levels of input from health and welfare services may have only a 'specificity of effect' – certain domains of an individual's life being changed for the better, whilst others remain unaffected.

In a quarter of a century of service to those suffering mental health problems, St Anne's has proved itself an alert and responsive organisation. As I have indicated, by drawing attention to the mission statement, the core activity has been the meeting of housing need. The service element of its work has been mindful of the need to cultivate choice and encourage autonomy among its users. By bringing these two elements together – housing and welfare support – the quality of life of mental health sufferers has been enhanced.

References

Baldwin, S., Godrey, C. and Propper, C. (1990) *Quality of Life: Perspectives and Policies.* London: Routledge.

Barham, P. (1992) *Closing the Asylum: The Mental Patient in Modern Society.* Harmondsworth: Penguin.

Barham, P. and Hayward, D. (eds) (1995) *Relocating Madness: From the Mental Patient to the Person.* London: Tavistock Routledge.

Barker, I. and Peck, E. (eds)(1987) *Power in Strange Places: User Empowerment in Mental Health Services.* London: Good Practices in Mental Health.

Bayliss, E. (1987) *Housing: The Foundation of Community Care.* London: National Federation of Housing Associations and MIND.

Butler, A., Oldman, C. and Greve, J. (1983) *Sheltered Housing for the Elderly: Policy, Practice and the Consumer.* London: Allen and Unwin.

Butler, A. and Pritchard, C. (1983) *Social Work and Mental Illness.* Basingstoke: Macmillan.

Clapham, D. and Smith, S. (1990) 'Housing policy and "special needs".' *Policy and Politics 18*, 3, 193–206.

Department of Health and Social Services (1971) *Hospital Services for the Mentally Ill.* London: HMSO.

Department of Health and Social Services (1975) *Better Services for the Mentally Ill.* Cmnd 6233. London: HMSO.

Hunt, S.M. (1990) 'Emotional distress and bad housing.' *Health and Hygiene 11*, 72–9.

Huxley, P. (1996) 'Quality of Life.' In K. Muesser and N. Tarrier (eds) *The Handbook of Social Functioning.* London: Addison-Wesley.

Hyndman, S.J. (1990) 'Housing, dampness and health among British Bengalis in East London.' *Social Science and Medicine 30*, 131–41.

Jolley, A., Hirsch, S. and Manchanda, R. (1989) 'Trial of brief intermittent neuroleptic prophylaxis for selected schizophrenic out-patients: clinical outcome at one year.' *British Medical Journal 289*, 985–90.

Jones, K. (1988) *Experience in Mental Health: Community Care and Social Policy.* London: Sage.

Kleinman, I., Schacter, D. and Koritar, E. (1989) 'Informed consent and tardive dyskinesia.' *American Journal of Psychiatry 146*, 7, 902–4.

Lawson, M. (1991) 'A recipient's view.' In S. Ramon (ed) *Beyond Community Care.* Basingstoke: Macmillan/MIND.

Lehman, A.F., Ward, N.C. and Lynn, L.S. (1982) 'Chronic mental patients: the quality of life issue.' *American Journal of Psychiatry 139*, 1271–6.

Lehman, A.F. (1988) 'A quality of life interview for the chronically mentally ill.' *Evaluation and Program Planning 11*, 51–62.

Leigh, C. (1994) *Everybody's Baby: Implementing Community Care for Single Homeless People.* London: CHAR.

Maslow, A. (1971) *The Farther Reaches of Human Nature.* London: Viking.

Means, R. (1987) 'Older people in British housing studies.' *Housing Studies 2*, 2, 82–98.

Means, R. and Smith, R. (1994) *Community Care: Policy and Practice.* Basingstoke: Macmillan.

MIND (1989) *Building Better Futures.* London: MIND Publications.

Ministry of Housing and Local Government (1969) *Housing Standards and Costs: Accommodation Designed for Old People*, Circular 82/69. London: HMSO.

Newton, J. (1992) *Preventing Mental Illness in Practice.* London: Routledge.

Oliver, J. and Butler, A. (1979) 'A living conditions rating scale (LCRS).' *International Social Work XXII*, 3, 27–38.

Oliver, J., Huxley, P., Bridges, K. and Mohamad, H. (1995) *Quality of Life and Mental Health Services.* London: Routledge.

Power, A. and Tunstall, R. (1995) *Swimming Against the Tide.* York: Joseph Rowntree Foundation.

Robertson, A. and Osborn, A. (1985) *Planning to Care – Social Policy and the Quality of Life.* London: ESRC.

Rogers, A. and Pilgrim, D. (1996) *Mental Health Policy in Britain.* Basingstoke: Macmillan.

Scull, A.T. (1977) *Decarceration: Community Treatment and the Deviant – A Radical View.* New Jersey: Prentice Hall.

Seebohm Report (1968) *Report of the Committee on Local Authority and Allied Personal Social Services,* Cmnd 3703. London: HMSO.

Townsend, P. (1962) *The Last Refuge.* London: Routledge and Kegan Paul.

Warner, R. (1985) *Recovery from Schizophrenia: Psychiatry and Political Economy.* London: Routledge and Kegan Paul.

Watson, L. and Cooper, R. (1992) *Housing with Care.* York: Joseph Rowntree Foundation.

Wheeler, R. (1988) 'Housing policy and elderly people.' In C. Phillipson and A. Walker (eds) *Ageing and Social Policy: A Critical Assessment.* Aldershot: Gower.

Wolfensberger, W. (1983) 'Social role valorization: a proposed new term for the principle of normalisation.' *Mental Retardation 21,* 234–9.

Wolfensberger, W. and Glenn, L. (1973) *Program Analysis of Service Systems (PASS) Handbook.* Toronto: National Institute in Mental Retardation.

Further reading

Clarke, M. and Stewart, J. (1992) 'Empowerment: a theme for the 1990s.' *Local Government Studies 18,* 2, 18–26.

Department of Health (1989) *Caring for People: Community Care in the Next Decade and Beyond.* London: HMSO.

Department of Health and Social Services Inspectorate (1991) *Care Management and Assessment: Summary of Practice Guidance.* London: HMSO.

Nuffield Provincial Hospitals Trust (1994) *Housing, Homelessness and Health.* London: NPHT.

CHAPTER 4

Community Care Policy

Quality of Life Issues in Housing Provision for People with Learning Disabilities

Nigel Malin

Background

Rationing and the search for a central purpose are a hallmark of the current debate in health and social care. *A Service With Ambitions*, the White Paper published in the dying days of the last government, had argued that pressures of demographic change, public expectation and medical advance were as manageable today as in the past. Such complacency merely fuels the contention that advancing the policy of community care has never been a political priority over the last four decades.

As yet there is no overall national strategy of either de-institutionalisation or community integration for the considerable number of people still in hospitals, hostels and large group homes who are caught up in the wake of (previous) liberal policies (Sinson, 1993). Following the introduction of the internal market in health and social care local 'provision' for people with learning disabilities has lost a special identity gained during the 1980s through emphasis on value-based services. Instead, much provision has become 'commodified' in response to market and economic forces. Services for people with learning disabilities are viewed in policy terms as part of community care in general and hence lack any sense of overall management or leadership.

Community care arising from de-institutionalisation

There exists no clear consensus regarding the forces driving the de-institutionalisation movement. The theme of the intellectual attack on institutional care is one in which other themes inevitably become interwoven. The claim was based upon theoretical work covering institutions, notably that of Goffman, Foucault, Szasz and British empiricists such as Russell Barton and Peter Townsend.

To take Goffman as example, his critique focused upon 'role dispossession'. He invented the concept of the 'total institution', contending that they have four main characteristics: batch living, binary management, the inmate role and the institutional perspective. 'Batch living' describes a situation where 'each phase of the member's daily activity is carried on in the immediate company of a large batch of others, all of whom are treated alike, and required to do the same thing together' (the mental hospital) (Goffman, 1961, p.6). His contention was that institutions have features in common. Not all features are specific to each institution but that this is the 'antithesis of individual living', contrasted with

> a basic arrangement in modern society [where] ... the individual tends to sleep, play and work in different places, with different co-participants under different authorities, and without an overall rational plan. (ibid., p.13)

How do ordinary people, with their own way of life and personal networks and round of activities, become inmates? Goffman thought that this is not a process of 'acculturation' which involves moving from one culture to another, but of 'disculturation' or 'role-stripping', so powerful that the individual who is subjected to it may be rendered incapable of normal living on return to the community. He/she has been reduced from a person with many roles to a cypher with one: the 'inmate role'. The central feature of a total institution was said to be a 'breakdown of the barriers' found in ordinary life normally separating the place to live, the place to work and the place for recreation.

The need for a 'culturally valued analogue' is one approach towards defining an alternative position, bearing in mind that as a concept community care appeared to be defined in terms of its opposition. The term may be deconstructed as dependent definitionally upon institutional care or care which is 'uncaring' and depersonalised or care provided less economically in hospitals. Whichever of these definitions is highlighted depends upon the interests of those using the term. This followed the line that long-stay institutions were harmful to patients and alternative settings in the community were preferable.

Research had been conducted on how adults with learning disabilities survived in the community with minimal support (Malin, 1983). Findings included that unlike previous residential placement, internal group behaviour factors affected the success or failure of group home placement, that changes in independent functioning and behaviour related to higher staff support, and the presence of neighbourhood and family had an explicit bearing on 'success' measured by extent of survival through non-return to hospital or hostel care. An earlier study had been undertaken in Glasgow studying staff attitudes and practices in both long-stay and community settings for people defined as having a learning disability (Malin, 1978). One recollection from this time was how services were isolated, lacking aims and professional leadership. Some nursing attitudes were that if they were not cruel or unkind to a patient then that was sufficient. There was little evidence of overall planning or vision nor focus upon individuals. The chief problem was articulated as how do people with learning disabilities get out of hospitals and obtain a better lifestyle. The policy of community care should not be viewed as sort of a continuum or metanarrative as, in reality, it is a changing set of assumptions owned by different groups, factions and political parties.

Community care arising from the 'planning for priority groups' movement in the 1970s

Most of the (central government) health and social services master plans published in the 1970s for client groups such as those with mental health problems, learning disabilities, and the elderly, took the view that community care could be planned rationally and incrementally through 'local agency collaboration' following general objectives and principles set up by central government. In retrospect this seems naive and ephemeral.

Other 'planning' assumptions were that there existed some kind of geographical grouping of people who were both able and willing to take on active caring on a consistent and reliable basis. This was despite the fact that the Seebohm Report (1968), which set up social service departments at that time, recognised the force of the argument that links between individuals who form a non-geographical 'community of interest' may be stronger than relationships made on the basis of locality.

In a study of the 1974 Labour government's attempts to redirect local health and social service resources to priority groups, the authors concluded that plans had not succeeded above all because 'the intellectual model for achieving change was simply inappropriate' (Glennerster and Lewis, 1996, p.20). Government had tried to adopt centralised, rational, comprehensive planning, had produced a national budget and planning guidelines; local districts and social service departments were intended to plan jointly to implement these guidelines. In practice, power in the NHS and local authorities was so diverse and the competing bureaucratic interests so entrenched that such a model had little hope of success.

To take the case of people with learning disabilities, the central government plan (Department of Health and Social Security, 1971) was gradually to decant hospitals over a 20-year period and place people in suitable smaller units in the community from where they could commute daily to various forms of day care. Between 1971 and 1991 around 1100 new places were to be provided in the community per annum as hospitals narrowed down. Table 4.1 gives a notion of the changing scale of events.

Although there is an approximate displacement from the health to the community sector numbers-wise, i.e. around 38,000 fewer places in hospital and an equivalent increase in the community, three things stand out:

E   the pace of change became more rapid during the last decade

E   the private sector of care opened up: a sevenfold increase in places
    between 1979 and 1995 (it is not only in provision for the elderly
    that the independent sector became the dominant partner)

E   around 26,000 places (roughly 65%) are still in facilities of 20+
    places (Emerson et al., 1996), i.e. 'institutional' or at least not an
    ordinary home, albeit 'in the community'.

In the case of mental health, a similar pattern over the last decade is evident, i.e. private provision in the community from 6,902 beds in 1987 to 12,245 (double) by 1995, with a decline in the number of hospital beds from 70,000 to just 40,000 over the same period. The number of local authority places during this period had dropped from 5,673 to 4,747. Tragically here it seems that much of the private provision are bedsits and squalid lodgings with non-existent care (landladies receiving money from social services). In the area of mental health since January 1996 there have been 24 inquiries into fatal incidents involving community care – each one costing around £250,000 and each one coming up with similar answers, similar lessons to be

Table 4.1 Residential places for adults with learning disabilities

	1969	1979	1985	1991		1995
				Projected number	Actual number	
NHS hospitals beds/places	52,100	45,400	41,000		20,074	11,400
				27,000		
Private nursing homes, hospitals			790		3,961	3,100
Local authority homes		11,400 staffed and unstaffed	11,100 (staffed)		12,978	9,670
Voluntary sector homes	4,300		3,180	29,400		13,960
Private residential homes		3,800 registered	2,950		16,181	12,730
Lodgings, foster homes	550			7,400		
Local authority unstaffed group homes			1,650			2,700
Small registered residential homes (less than 4 places, voluntary/private)						2,470
						Total: 56,030

learned and recommendations. The overall point is that people have been gradually moved out since the 1970s but not into 'community care' in the true sense, or necessarily more personal, homelike care.

The gender debate

The third strand in the galaxy is the gender debate, or rather the mode by which community care policy has become re-examined in response to the carers' lobby.

Jill Manthorpe (1994) observed that

> women's compulsory altruism is potentially damaging to themselves [which] may disregard the perspectives of those who receive their support as compulsory dependents. (p.101)

In the last decade or so influential studies from feminist writers have played a key part in community care developments and have dominated the agenda. The principal outcome has been the Carers Recognition Act (1995) which provides recognition of assessment and independent consideration of their position in terms of their own needs for help and support.

These studies have shown how carers form the bedrock of policy and that they are exploited. At the root of all community care policies seems to be the firm belief that the family is the appropriate unit and location of care. Privacy and independence – both regarded as being goals to be prized and achieved – can best be secured by remaining in one's own home. The family, it is believed, has a moral duty to care; the bosom of the family is the place where a dependent person ought to be; the state should keep out of the essentially private business of caring wherever possible. So the argument goes.

This argument has received a very high profile – it has challenged the need for 'professional' care. The late Sir Roy Griffiths, whose report *Community Care: An Agenda for Action* (1988) formed the basis of the current National Health Service and Community Care Act, took this further by arguing for the creation of a new occupation of carers to undertake 'the frontline personal and social support of dependent people' (para 8.4), a sort of direct attack on the need for expensive professional care.

How to 'empower' carers has become central to the gender-based debate. Yet more recently this idea has run into conflict with the discourse on citizenship and empowerment struck on behalf of disabled people themselves. In a recent paper, Clare Ungerson (1997) has demonstrated the paradox (the inherent tension) that the growth in power of one group (i.e. carers) implicitly means that power is being redistributed and there are other groups who are – or should be – losing ground. Part of the implicit purpose of the new community care regime was to clip the wings of powerful professionals in the health and social care fields who were previously wedded to 'service-led' rather than 'needs-led' provision for people with special needs. This has become recently manifest in the new (April 1997) Direct Payments legislation whereby disabled people will be able to opt for cash rather than services and become employers of personal assistants.

In learning disabilities the gender debate has incorporated oral history research (Atkinson and Williams, 1990; Walmsley, 1993) indicating contradictions, particularly in relation to caring. Writers such as Hilary Graham (1983) have shown that being in a position to offer care to others can also be seen as something many women value as an expression of female identity. Whereas caring can be a means by which (non-disabled) women enter the public world, these opportunities do not necessarily transfer to women with learning disabilities who may find that informal and domestic caring at home effectively traps them in the private sphere (Williams, 1992).

The mixed economy or internal market model of community care policy

This model, which constitutes the basis of the present reforms, is a feature of our times and represents the way by which governments have sought to check the growth of state social security spending through the explicit announcement of a policy on care in the community. The real interests of government are camouflaged through rhetoric on the rights of people to remain in the community and to have their needs assessed.

Driven by the desire to curb local health and welfare spending and to make previously sacrosanct agencies like parts of the NHS more accountable, the government introduced the internal market with the aim of offering extended choice and giving freedom to a plethora of providers from the independent/private sector who would challenge orthodoxy, the professions and their collective right to provide health care. A further purpose was to make more visible the price of transactions, to cut waste and reduce power of constituent providers.

Glennerster and Lewis (1996) distinguish between the deep normative core of a policy, the near core and secondary aspects. The last can be changed by local actors whilst the policy still achieves its basic objectives. Reducing the growth of state social security spending was the normative core, the real heart of the government's policy, referring to the way by which central government had inadvertently during the 1980s continued to subsidise without discretion the cost of private residential and nursing care.

Creating a mixed market where the local authorities moved from their dominant provider role to an enabling role and encouraging collaboration between health and social services were near core policies in the sense that the government could be somewhat relaxed about the way they were implemented. Forms of assessment and individual client care management and care planning were secondary to the government's main purposes. Deterritorialising dependency relations between carer and cared-for and the potential of a new conception of care as facilitation and empowerment where professionals reorientate their roles (away) from expertise towards facilitation was how one observer described the changes (Fox, 1993).

The rhetoric of the reforms has taken on a language of its own, such as:

E 'seamless' (DoH, 1990, para 1.9) – that the user should not be aware of any divisions between health and social services

E 'spectrum of care' – a range of choice befitting the consumer

E (the evolution of) 'quasi-markets' – the need to map out and stimulate a large number of providers and purchasers of care, all the responsibilities of enabling authorities

E 'commodification' – referring to fundholding budget contribution units (otherwise known as patients!).

Evidence over the last four years up and down the country suggests that expansion of the internal market has provoked a measure of chaos and turmoil where litigation cases have ensued over debating a person's right to a service alongside that of an agency's concomitant defence over not having to provide it (witness the case of Gloucester County Council in 1996). Handing over parts of residential and domiciliary care to the private sector has in many instances lowered standards, reduced or removed training, lowered wages for careworkers and led to further litigation (witness the case in Cornwall reported in *Guardian*, 21 April 1997). There is now a ruling that a provider taking over from a council cannot dismiss and re-employ staff on lower rates.

Similarly a recent report covering a selection of homes mainly in the private sector published by Bright (1997) has suggested the need for much firmer tightening up of the powers of the independent inspectorate in the light of more reported cases of physical and emotional abuse. It further recommends that care homes are required to display a notice detailing with whom staff can safely raise concerns with. The Nolan Committee has ruled that local authorities need to institute codes of practice on 'whistleblowing' – encouraging staff to expose abuse. This is not to suggest that all private is bad and public sector provision superior, but the increase in reported cases and the greater media criticism implies that much is occurring that goes unnoticed.

The impact of politicising community care has strengthened the arm of managers. In learning disabilities one set of authors (Emerson, Mansell and

McGill, 1994) has referred to this as the 'metaphor of production' – where the house or work or school placement can be thought of as a production system – as a kind of machine. The product the service makes is the lifestyle experience by the service user, and the task of the innovator is to construct a service which can deliver this outcome; quality of life being such an outcome. So far the argument has been that more than one form of discourse has influenced the history of community care, but there does not appear to be any overarching unity or theory supporting the scale of charges.

In the absence of theory?

Social theorists now disclaim romantic attachment to any erstwhile 'family-' or 'community-' based model of care inherited from the past. It is now fashionable to state as fabrication to discern in community care an ideology which draws some of its potency from an imagined past in which aged, handicapped and sick were cared for in family or neighbourhood groupings. The argument is that there has been a move away from familial relationships grounded in rights, duties and responsibilities towards commodified relations – less personal, less loyal, less flexible and more controlled – as a consequence of the rise of post-industrial society.

On policy the three main political parties in their (1997) pre-election manifestos stressed few, if any, commitments: more partnership with the private sector, more inspection, charters and standards, but no overall programme that was specific. The new Labour government has been accused of putting decisions about how to deal with the thorny issue of long-term care on the back-burner with its plan to pass the task of deciding how to fund and provide it to a Royal commission. (We note also its recent decision to scrap the full-time post of Minister for the Disabled.) The Conservatives intended (at least according to their manifesto) to extend the direct payments scheme to other users and keep long-stay mental hospitals open until adequate care services became available in the community, whereas the Liberal Democrats would have introduced a carers' benefit. It seems reasonable to regard such policies as piecemeal since they fail to indicate any central strategy.

In learning disabilities the context of normalisation has provided a valuable driving force. Here the starting point tends to be the roles that people occupy rather than people as the persons they are. Wolfensberger's (1972) reformulation of the principle of normalisation around a Lemertian social deviance perspective stressed the importance of the role of ideology in the way human service organisations are structured. He described the dynamics underlying society's attitudes to devalued groups through the process of labelling; that is people are devalued because they are labelled as deviant.

To be categorised as deviant may mean that such individuals are seen variably as menaces, subhuman, childlike, diseased, ridiculous. He viewed services as operating at both a conscious and unconscious level, conditioning the way society and its professional agents think and behave. Normalisation contains an ideological imperative which stresses the need to reverse this process of social devaluing. His much-quoted definition of normalisation has been a fixture:

> the utilisation of means which are as culturally normative as possible, in order to establish and/or maintain personal behaviours and characteristics which are as culturally normative as possible (pp.18–42).

Normalisation has been criticised for its conservatism, its moral authoritarianism and conformism. Gillian Dalley (1992), for example, stressed instead a collectivist approach advocating values of mutual support, cooperation and equality of status for all citizens as being more likely to nurture devalued people than the individualist tendencies of Wolfensberger's normalisation. A main argument against normalisation is that ideology is more significant than Wolfensberger appears to imply – that is, if society is to offer people valued roles then there must be a fundamental re-evaluation of those categories of persons qua persons. Also that there is need to address as a higher priority those forces within society which disempower, devalue and categorise people (rather than the people themselves).

Normalisation offers an explanation but does not go all the way: it implies a level of blame towards disabled individuals and works at reconstituting them into valued citizens (a societal approach). It has however been immensely significant in the last two decades in forwarding policy on closing down old hospitals and supporting change to an ordinary life.

Quality of life and the person-centred approach

This has become an important conceptual paradigm in evaluating services. Writers have variously described it as elusive and multidimensional (Michalos, 1976; Felce and Perry, 1993). According to Liu (1976) there are as many quality of life definitions as there are people. There are two separate phenomena:

E quality of life

E satisfaction with life.

The first is the summation of a range of objectively assessed life conditions as experienced by an individual, for example, physical health, material wealth, social relationships; the second is the subjective response to such conditions, i.e. level of personal satisfaction with life. Researchers in learning disabilities have argued that the concept of quality of life must combine both objective and subjective components, that is the interaction of life conditions with personal values and life satisfaction (Emerson, 1985; Felce and Perry, 1993).

In the event, quality of life is now a phrase used to accommodate policy objectives and to provide eclectic impressions of circumstances of individuals in the community – it has been less useful in measuring real change in the lives of such individuals. Services may be able to provide examples where choice, privacy and opportunity appear to have been enhanced by moving people to a community residential home, but it is not clear whether they are simply describing general changes within the physical environment or changes in life conditions as actually experienced by the clients themselves.

Recent research on quality of life in ordinary housing for adults with learning disabilities shows variable results, for example, short- rather than long-term changes in residents' behaviour meaning that the service is successful in maintaining a level of improvement but not in moving beyond it. Also found have been persistent low levels of service-user involvement in meaningful activity and low levels of staff–client interaction stressing 'failure to fully realise the opportunities created by the abandonment of institutions' (Emerson et al. 1994; Felce, 1996; Mansell and Ericsson, 1996).

This suggests that it is the way in which staff work with service users rather that the way staffed housing is set up that is responsible. There is now considerable evidence from the literature that 'ordinary' housing has taken on distinctively institutional characteristics, that this does not necessarily translate into a wider range of significant relationships and that, despite all the rhetoric, these are not services based on the needs of individuals (Simons, 1997).

St Anne's Shelter & Housing Action is based in Leeds and runs around 50–60 supported housing units for adults with learning disabilities chiefly in West and North Yorkshire. Partly to find out how care staff perceived quality of life, groups of staff from each house were asked to complete questionnaires looking at two issues: providing examples of individuals whose quality of life had changed (for better or for worse) since moving to the home (how and in what way changes had occurred); and identifying factors responsible for such changes.

Twenty-eight questionnaires were completed. Examples given stressed more activity geared to independent living, drawing out contrasts with institutional life. Staff made judgements based largely, it seemed, on the perceived availability of greater opportunities for residents, rarely on evidence taken from the clients themselves. The following presents answers to the first question taken directly from the questionnaires.

Staff perceptions of individuals whose quality of life has changed as a result of moving 'into the community'

> X is 39 and lived in a large institution from the age of 15 until 1990 when she moved with five other people to a purpose-built bungalow. This person now has regular outings and enjoys them, relatives are able to visit more frequently, there is more personal space and more opportunity to practice personal and self-help skills. They are able to have regular activities which can be planned for in advance as there are less residents in the house and one-to-one staffing is easier to arrange than on a hospital ward. Medical care is from a GP service and doesn't always take on a psychological slant. Access to specialists seems easier using this system than it did in hospitals.

* * *

> W moved to supported housing little more than a year ago. Prone to regular moodiness, irritability, difficult and sometimes aggressive behaviour in residential care, W has developed whilst in supported housing a sense of contentment as his confidence in managing himself has grown. This is reflected by his gradually diminishing obsessions with his health. Issues of personal care and diet are still problematic.

* * *

> Since coming to live here (from an institution) D is able to go out in the garden when he feels like it. He is also taken on public transport which never happened before and mixes with other people at college. If D had not come to live in the community he would not have had the experiences he has had. He is able to mix quite socially now and table manners have improved immensely. D has learned how to socially interact with others and has learned how to wait, which was a big problem when he first came to live here.

* * *

> In the first year of living at Heatherstones one of our clients exhibited and had a history of self-injurious behaviour and required a wrap to act as

a comforter to reduce self-injurious behaviour. This client no longer wears the wrap and incidents of self-injurious behaviour are less. The level of self-injurious behaviour and wearing the wrap were not conducive to social integration. This client now lives an active social life and has adjusted to having the same values as us, i.e. going shopping in town, having dinner in town, out for holidays at valued locations. Noticeably the client's personal skills have enhanced.

★ ★ ★

Of the seven clients living at Cloughside, six were of the local disability hospital prior to its closure. Most of the house staff had worked with them for a number of years and in effect we all moved out together. At the hospital, clients lived in an emotionally and physically impaired environment with extremely limited choices. The culture was one of control which encouraged liberal use of chemical cosh. The aim of the staff was to 'keep the lid from blowing' in the hope of better days to come. Consider the opposite of the above situation and compare the lifestyle that those people now have – I feel you won't find an awful lot of difference: personal bedrooms (single), greater personal monies (via benefits, particularly DCA), increased choices in all walks of life, including having the power to say no, far better food etc. The list could go on for much longer than this but perhaps the most important aspect is that staff/carers now have the opportunity (time, numbers, philosophy) to regard those people as individuals and to respond to them as such.

★ ★ ★

The gentleman had previously spent over forty years of his life living in a hospital setting, with all the dehumanising practices associated with institutions. The gentleman showed all his anger and frustration within this environment with ripping his own clothing, and physically attacking his peers and staff. He was looked upon as a person 'who portrays behaviours which challenge the service'. He moved to his new home over three years ago. The home is on a quiet cul-de-sac in a small town. Over the last three years he has stopped ripping his own clothing and does not assault the other two gentlemen that he lives with or the staff that support him in his home. The gentleman's quality of life has developed by him having his own space, bedroom, living areas which has enabled him to express his own individuality. He now has opportunities to make choices over small everyday occurrences, what clothes to wear, what food to eat, what music to listen to, and issues of a social nature, where to go on an evening and with whom and regaining family contacts. During the last three years the gentleman's lifestyle has broadened, offering more choice and control in day-to-day issues within and out of the home environment.

★ ★ ★

The person I am discussing had spent some thirty years of large institutionalised living before coming under the auspices of St Anne's eight years ago. The obvious benefits that E has experienced since living in the community is an improvement in his living environment. Instead of living in large, contained, largely populated institutional buildings, E now lives in a respected neighbourhood which allows him to play an integral part within the community. Because community living provides easier access and opportunity to public facilities, i.e. public transport, libraries, parks, E can now enjoy visiting different venues, thus widening and enriching his life. Another area that has been of benefit to E is the pride he displays in his personal living accommodation. Instead of a room filled with institutional fitments, he has been able to furnish and equip his room with belongings of his own choice and he also enjoys the privacy that this gives him. E's quality of life has changed quite dramatically in many ways: it has allowed him greater personal development, greater independence, choice of interests and differing situations he wants to experience. The facility of a key worker allows him to pursue these areas, on a one-to-one basis, rather than part of a large group – which encourage normalisation which community living promotes.

★ ★ ★

1. There is no longer the large grounds which provided more freedom of movement without staff [negative].
2. There is not as much abuse (by other residents) as there was at Whixley. There is more time to communicate and develop personalities [positive].

★ ★ ★

F is a 54-year-old woman who has been in care since the age of ten. She moved from a large psychiatric hospital into a small nursing home in the community approximately seven years ago. F shares a home with five other people, whereas there were nineteen other people in the same hospital ward. She therefore receives far more attention from staff now than she used to. F did not appear to like to the personal contact with people before, but now that staff can spend more time with her individually she appears more confident in company and more sociable. F preferred not to take part in occupational activities in the hospital but now attends the day centre for four sessions a week, appearing to enjoy the personal attention and watching the activities around her. She also attends discos and parties. One area which has been improved considerably is the amount of privacy F has. She now has her own room with personal belongings. The toilet and bathing facilities are also much better. There are three separate toilets in the bungalow she lives in now, plus another in the bathroom, whereas before there were only four toilet cubicles in a row, with a number of commodes in a common washroom.

Bathing is also private now, but rather hectic before with staff getting 20 people bathed or washed and dressed in one bathroom containing two baths, and one washroom. This had to be done by a certain time as breakfast was delivered from the hospital kitchens, and the tins and trays etc. had to be returned to the kitchen to be washed and used for the next meal. The atmosphere at meal times can be more relaxed now. There is also more flexibility with mealtimes as main meals and snacks can be altered to fit in with daytime activities rather that kept to a rigid time. In the more homely atmosphere F helps with a few domestic tasks, e.g. taking crockery, glasses back to the kitchen at the end of mealtimes.

★ ★ ★

An elderly lady with a mild learning difficulty: the lady lived in a hostel accommodation in Ripon for seven or eight years. During this time she relied on staff from the hostel or other residents, to facilitate her usage of Ripon (shops, cafes, public houses etc.). This lady then moved in 1987 to smaller accommodation housing ten people with learning disabilities and was then encouraged to become more independent. In 1993 this lady then moved to a smaller group home housing five people with learning disabilities. The encouragement to become more independent continued with the key worker and all members of the staff team doing risk assessments etc. on independent use of local transport and taxis. This lady is now able to visit Ripon independently using local transport and taxis and visits shops and cafes where she has made many new friends.

★ ★ ★

Lady DOB 15/08/31. Virtually no speech very poor mobility. Lived in a long-stay hostel for people with learning difficulties. Had very little private space, small bedroom, little time for a bath, lots of 'block treatments', i.e. mealtimes, getting up and going to bed when told etc., clothes brought in bulk, outings in large groups. Now lives in a five-bedroomed house, but very much a home. Loves a long leisurely bath and dresses herself, enjoys days out on a one-to-one basis, chooses own clothes and holidays etc. At nighttime she will sit up in bed watching her own television (having a glass of sherry). Brought her own furniture for the room and is involved in all discussions relating to her life. At her first review she cried because it was the first time she had been consulted about her wishes.

★ ★ ★

D's life, I feel has changed for the better as a result of living in the community. I personally worked with D at Fieldhead Hospital where he was on a villa with over 23 at any given time all with physical disabilities or severe learning disabilities. The villa was staffed with three at the very most. Very few residents ever went out and only the more capable went on holiday as staffing did not allow for this, D's daily routine was to be dressed in hospital issue clothes and sit in his wheelchair ready for breakfast, having to wait until all 23 were dressed. Breakfast was a rush to feed 23 residents, after which he was sat on an easy chair (communal). He did not have nappies so when incontinent he was changed as his clothes would be wet or dirty. Clothes went to the hospital laundry and were often ruined or lost. D did not attend any activities or training, none were available at the time (1984). D's day was sat in a chair with television or radio and occasional walk only if staff permitted. Bathtime was communal bathroom with three other baths so he did not have much privacy even though he had a bath everyday. He also shared a bedroom with four others. Now D has his own bedroom and his own CD system which he enjoys. He has a more comfortable wheel chair brought out of his own money. D now attends many activities which keep him happy and has at least one holiday a year with one-to-one staffing. He lives in a house with five other residents which is usually staffed with at least two staff. He attends the day centre on a regular basis and goes to hydrotherapy. He has days out, meals out, visits, walks etc. Now D has an IIP which highlights his needs and how we should achieve these, where however, in the past there was not much of a system. D's quality of life has improved immensely since coming into the community. We are still looking for some outside activity for D to participate with.

* * *

P is 44 years old. He has severe learning difficulties and is blind in both eyes. P can walk with some help, though he needs help with most daily tasks, but can understand most instructions. P can communicate verbally but cannot talk. P lives in Oxfield Court with five other people with similar learning difficulties. P leads a comfortable life where his needs are well catered for. He has lived in Oxfield Court since December 1991. Before then he lived at Fieldhead Hospital where he had spent most of his life. When P first lived at Oxfield his feeding skills were fairly limited. He would use his fingers to pick up his food, sometimes he would put his plate to his mouth. He would also regurgitate most of his meal after he had eaten. This problem made it difficult for him to take part in the community. It was difficult to take P to restaurants or public houses due to the regurgitation. Gradually P improved his feeding skills. This was achieved by devising feeding programmes which all the staff carried out. A special chair was purchased which enabled P to sit up straight therefore making regurgitation more difficult. Six years later and P now sits at the table with other residents and feeds himself with just a little bit of help. This great improvement to P's skills meant that his life has improved quite a bit. P can now enjoy meals out, overnight stays, holidays and more importantly cuddles which he missed out on before due to his unpleasant smells and messy clothes. P has also benefited from his 'snoezelen' room which he enjoys and has relaxed in. This room has special lighting, comfy mats and cushions and music to stimulate his hearing and sight senses. P's life has also benefited from activities at the day centre and the use of a hydrotherapy pool when it is turned on. P has always had a good relationship with his mum, she now lives more locally since P moved to Oxfield, their bond is very close. P's mum is very happy with his current standard of living and improved life skills, she says that she has really noticed an improvement.

* * *

Because D was classed as a person with challenging behaviour, he was in a locked ward and was not allowed out on his own. Since coming to live here he is able to go out in the garden when he feels like it. He is also taken on public transport which never happened before. D mixes with other people at college etc. If D had not come to live in the community he would not have had the experience he has had. He is able to mix quite socially now and table manners have improved immensely. D has learned to be socially involved with others and learned how to socially interact with others and has learned to wait, which was a big problem when he first came to live here.

* * *

The client has lived in the community for four years in a bungalow divided into two homes which was designed for seven people. The client resides with two other clients and now has her own room, with many personal possessions, material items and good quality clothing. The nursing home is staffed by RMNH and nursing assistants and there are three/four staff on duty during the day and two at night. Clients are respected as individuals and are given choices and are treated with dignity. The client now has more opportunities for community participation and 'normal living' and now uses the same services and facilities as others, such as GP, dentist, chemist, hairdresser. The client goes out three times a week for very varied leisure pursuits and activities such as swimming, shopping, meals out, funfairs, flying in aeroplanes. The client also enjoys successful, individual holidays twice a year with two staff members and is regularly visited by family and friends who have now become friends of the staff. The client has also become less solitary, and now seeks interaction with others and has good personal relationships with staff. It appears that the client would benefit from more personal space as the home and garden is smaller than previous places of residence.

* * *

S's quality of life has been seen to improve in many areas. S really enjoys being in the kitchen cooking and of course in hospital this was regarded as impractical or dangerous. However, through trial and error S has gained enough confidence to prepare and cook the food that she alone enjoys – after of course choosing it in the supermarket. S now regards the kitchen as somewhere to learn, where giant Yorkshire puds and butterfly buns come out of the oven. S was amazed the first time she turned margarine, sugar, eggs and flour into paper cases and produced buns – rather than finding them on a plate ready for tea. S now knows how they got there. However, because S has learnt so much and has an enquiring mind, it can cause problems as her learning difficulties sometimes prevent her from following things through to their conclusion. There was an example where S took £5 to buy toiletries in Boots, convinced she had enough in her purse for about 30 quid's worth of stuff.

★ ★ ★

The chance to establish a close personal relationship (boyfriend/ girlfriend) whilst living next door to each other in their own flats after leaving residential care, eventually leading to marriage and a joint flat.

★ ★ ★

The chance to establish relationships in the local community – family, friends, neighbours, shop staff, health care workers etc.

★ ★ ★

Financial independence through benefits; the chance to save and make more choices in their lives about household furniture and furnishings, clothes, leisuretime activities and holidays.

★ ★ ★

W is a woman in her late 50s who has lived in supported housing for over seven years. Always difficult to work with, W was moody and mistrustful and prior to my own time working with her was evidently developing mental health problems with delusions and paranoia. Shortly after starting work with W, she had a breakdown and was sectioned for six weeks. Since then and after the prescription of antipsychotic drugs, W's condition has improved enormously. Her mood is now stable and very content. Her delusions have diminished and are rarely expressed. She is much more outgoing and is beginning to develop real relationships with people.

★ ★ ★

M has Down's syndrome. She is a very endearing little lady with quite a character when you get to know her. When she first came here to live she was like a little mouse, hardly spoke and couldn't put more than two words together. She would have been quite capable of sitting in a corner all day on her own, if left. Gradually M gained more confidence and would help with the washing up and dusting, loved to help to bake, used to say she had been 'cooooking'. She used to sing a lot, loved the old songs and as her confidence increased so did her character develop. M became quite impish, and full of fun. M attended the ATC each day and really loved going, especially with her regular bus driver. Whilst living here M had a holiday each year, she went twice to Euro Disney which she thought was wonderful. M was encouraged to choose her own clothes and really let her opinion show. Putting clothes in drawers in her bedroom was a novelty, she liked to rummage through them a lot and did get quite possessive about them. Unfortunately just after her 60th birthday party – which she thoroughly enjoyed, she loved parties – M started with a mental illness. She developed various phobias and would not go upstairs or outside. It eventually became impossible to keep her in this house which was now her home without the necessary facilities. Fortunately there was bed available in a nursing home for people with special needs belonging to St Anne's and in the same area, so M moved there. Although living in this house did not work out for M in the long term she did live her for about six years, I'm sure these were happy ones.

* * *

A has become more confident and self-assured since her move to this small home. She happily performs many domestic tasks and is a proud owner of her own bedroom, which she never had before. A takes part in activities such as 'Bright Hour', is a regular attender, mixing with local people, she also goes to ATC, and uses local shops independently.

* * *

Mr S lived in a large, long-stay hospital prior to his discharge into St Anne's Shelter & Housing scheme's care. Whilst he does not have the use of speech, this is often considered to be far too loud, often impossible to understand and irrelevant to his everyday life and experiences. He also has a longstanding problem of refusing to eat and finding mealtimes stressful. Since moving to St Anne's care, this situation has begun to change. On one occasion in a local supermarket when he spotted a popular brand of chocolate bar, saying it's name and putting it in the trolley. In a local public house, when asked what he would like to drink, he asked for orange juice. After receiving still orange, he returned to the bar and made it clear that he wanted 'fresh orange juice'. In similar ways he has enabled his carers to understand his particular likes and dislikes in food, drink, music and many other areas of his life. As his language has become more meaningful his confidence and ambition have also grown.

* * *

The gentleman who I am discussing is about 43 years old and has a moderate learning disability, he spent many years living in various institutions. Although he appeared happy enough in this environment, when you actually looked at his life and life experiences they were very limited. There were so many things he had never done, never been on a train, never been into a restaurant, never had his own room, never had a proper holiday, this list just goes on. So from the very early stages of moving into a small home his quality of life increased, and the processes of giving him new adventures began. As time went on a totally different person began to emerge, he realised that he could say something and be heard and he could decide what he wanted to say or not as the case may be.

★ ★ ★

1. From sitting all day in front of a television screen, rejecting all social or physical contact with others, by biting and nipping everyone in reaching distance, refusing to leave the chair to go out, all this leads to the person being ignored and never going out. Then developing into an extremely sociable person who is first to collect his coat to go out; very few incidents of biting and nipping; increased and improved mobility, pleasant to be with well liked and respected.

★ ★ ★

2. From a person who could roam freely around large grounds, visit various areas / departments and individuals as and when, returning for meals and drinks at choice. Then developing into a person who is restricted indoors or a small garden unless a member of staff is available to go further afield, resulting in extremely aggressive behaviour towards himself and others around him.

★ ★ ★

An 80-year-old gentleman who had been in various institutions since the age of two. Living in London area before being exchanged for a patient in North Yorkshire. He had been living in a community home for nearly nine years. In this time his life has changed greatly for the better. His communication skills have been improved. He enjoys community life, meeting people in his local area, going to the shop, barbers, restaurants, always having money in his purse. His own bedroom furnishings to call his own. Having the choice of when he gets up, goes to bed and when he has his meals, and can have as much tea as he likes.

★ ★ ★

Mr G has a better quality of life as a result of community living. He doesn't like to go out a lot but is much happier in his new home. He walks now but, wouldn't do so in the past. His living skills are greatly improved. A few years ago, he wouldn't tolerate people near him and could become aggressive if people invaded his space, but he will now approach staff for appropriate affection. Because he walks all day, following staff, his physical condition is greatly improved. Mr G is much happier and more content, maybe because there are no longer large, noisy groups to be a threat to him.

* * *

Mr B lived in Meanwood Park Hospital from the age of five years. He moved into a residential care home of St Anne's in April 1988 where he lived with two other men. He was taught by staff at a local college to enable him to have new basic living skills for life in the community. Mr B started attending a local church where he met a lady who had been in care with him as a small child. The relationship began to grow, but in 1992 it was decided that the house where he was living would be given over to a different client group. Mr B had now got himself well established in the local community, attending college, church and the training centre. He had also made many new friends who visited him at the house. So Mr B said that he did not want to leave the area that he had, with help, made his community, to live in the area he was offered. At this time housing supported flats were being built in the area for St Anne's. No one was sure how or if this would be possible, but with help from staff and all his new friends this was made possible in 1993. Soon Mr B grew more confident in all his newfound skills also his relationship with Miss S grew. In July 1995 Mr B and Miss S became Mr and Mrs B and they go on from strength to strength. This year they will be going on their first holiday abroad and this gives me such great pleasure as I was in at the beginning of Mr B's move into the community, and know in my post as housing support worker I see just how excellent they are, complementing each other. Mr B has recently celebrated his 50th birthday.

* * *

Advantages of living in a community: (1) A woman at home with her family moved in two friends who also have a learning disability when her family moved away from the area. This enabled her stay at home and live more independently, therefore keeping regular contact with the family. (2) A gentleman moved into a small residential home ten years ago after living at home with his parents. Making an independent step away from his parents and avoiding institutional establishments. He continues to live with two friends and minimal staff support. (3) A resident participated in a leisure pursuit (horse-riding). At first staff gave her attention supporting her through the whole activity. Gradually she became more confident and skilful. Now she travels to and from horse riding independently using access transport. She manages her finances and she arrives to pay for her lesson, and her ability to ride the horse has steadily progressed to the point where she can leave the arena and walk in the woods carrying out various exercises, like balancing with her hands on her head. (4) A resident moved to the community from a long-stay hospital, she is encouraged to join in community activities and has also had the opportunity to go to Meanwood Park Hospital's tearoom on Saturdays to keep in touch with friends. (5) A resident works two days a week in a local supermarket, earning a wage and building a life for himself, with two friends in the community. (6) A resident in paid employment four days a week is keen to take holidays up to three times a year.

Disadvantages of living in a community: (1) Limited care provided in one house as residents are able to prepare light snacks, use the telephone and secure the building. However, problems do arise with local residents and children when staff are not on duty. (2) A female resident moved from a long-stay hospital with large grounds. Her new home in the community has many advantages however, she can no longer independently walk around outside as the home is next to a busy road and the garden very small. Garden furniture is regularly being replaced due to theft.

★ ★ ★

Mr X used to spend most of his time standing at a ward window, when in hospital, he now has a lot more freedom, more independence, his speech has increased, and he is now more content.

Bb – his background: Bb lived with his parents and his brother until his early teens. He was then admitted to the Fieldhead Hospital, the last learning disabilities hospital to be opened in the country, and was thought to be at the forefront of provision for this client group. Bb remained at Fieldhead hospital for a considerable period of time – until the early 1980s – when he was transferred to the mansion at Storthes Hall Hospital. He remained there for only a short period of time before his transfer back to Fieldhead. This time the stay was brief, Bb being one of the first people to take up residence in the newly opened Queensway in Kirkburton which continues to remain his home. Bb – the person: Bb is a quiet gentleman who has good verbal communications skills and is able to articulate his needs, but who on a frequent basis can be quite repetitive in his requests. Bb is able to dress with a little supervision from staff, although unable to see to his personal hygiene needs. At mealtimes, Bb is able to use a knife and fork appropriately, but this is an area where his skills have deteriorated recently.

★ ★ ★

Bb likes going to church, visiting churches and cathedrals, trips to old cities like York or Chester, having his own bedroom, television, and piano music.

Bb dislikes sports and shopping.

Bb skills: Bb is able to play piano and organ, and read simple music scores.

Institutional living: Sleeping in a dormitory with at least ten other residents. Lack of space for keeping and displaying personal belongings. They are also open from abuse by other residents. Personal clothing sent to hospital laundry which are often ruined or appearance greatly altered. Mealtimes were very impersonal and lacking imagination. There were no opportunities to develop skills and be involved in mealtimes. Entertainment and social life were very restrictive – tended to focus inward to the hospital. Residents often went out in large groups which reinforced the stigma which can be associated with a person with learning disabilities. Poor staff-resident ratio which meant that residents had minimal one-to-one attention from staff. Staff often lacked drive and motivation to support residents leading as full life as possible.

> Facilities for bathing and washing lacked privacy and dignity one would expect in one's own home. Involvement from relatives and carers was very limited. There was no privacy for visiting relatives. Relatives not consulted or involved with care plans. Residents not involved in choosing or buying their personal clothes.

Life in the community: Own bedroom with own personal belongings, individual bedding, which is more in keeping with a home environment. Better facilities for washing and ironing personal clothes. Given a choice of meals. Mealtimes are more flexible to accommodate residents' needs. Entertainment and social life are very varied and adapted to Bb's needs and interest ie church, concerts, day trips etc. Bb has developed a social network surrounding the church, with volunteers collecting him for church services. He attends church functions and is accepted as part of the community. Staff and resident ratio is better. More individual work is done to enable them to be a person first and someone with learning disabilities second.

Bb leads a 'normal' life, accessing general health services as you or I may, e.g. being registered with a local GP, visiting the chiropodist at the health centre, using a local dentist. Facilities for bathing and washing are greatly improved, the privacy of individuals being at the forefront. Bb has an individual programme plan which is reviewed annually.

Bb's family are given the opportunity to be involved. If relatives or friends visit, they are made to feel welcome and are encouraged to participate in the activities of the home, i.e. parties, mealtimes. Bb goes shopping and chooses his own clothes.

Bb's quality of life has enabled him to be a person in his own right, using community facilities as you and I would, where his learning disability is seen not as a handicap. He is now living his life to his full potential.

Staff perceptions of factors which have brought about the changes described

As to factors giving rise to such changes, overwhelmingly support and encouragement by staff was cited as the reason – 'as X now lives in a much smaller group, she no longer has to compete for staff attention … staff can take the time to listen', as one staff member put it. Another example: 'Staff have been able to spend more quality time with B to help him to develop his skills and learn new ones' (staff member). Apart from the environmental benefits available by moving to a small community home, the question of the style and effectiveness of care and support remains rather nebulous. That is to say, relatively little is known about which methods and practices work and which do not. Problem solving in professional practice has not been subject to any kind of detailed evaluation.

> The client now lives in a house shared by two other clients and needs are better assessed, met and evaluated at Heatherstones. The client has more choice and work is directed to social competence. The client's medical needs have been better met, i.e. need for HRT because of age. The key worker relationship has had a synergistic reaction with the client and has brought out quality of care and confidence for the client. The client's general appearance is very different.

★ ★ ★

> Time spent with S on a one-to-one basis – feeling that the kitchen is 'hers' and therefore feels relaxed and confident making a mess or whatever. S's own willingness to learn in her 'new life' outside the institution. Having a 'normal' domestic setting and not a large industrial kitchen and equipment. The fact that S has her own money and can independently purchase whatever toiletries she wants and knows which shops to go to after staff have discussed issues surrounding shops and money.

★ ★ ★

> The support they both received initially which allowed them to access benefits and financial independence. The support to help them manage their own tenancies and now the joint tenancy. Money management; shopping; cleaning; accessing health care. The support that allowed them both to make their own choice, without just seeing the difficulties that such a choice for a couple with learning disabilities would entail.

* * *

W had for a long time been wanting to move into his own flat, but each time the issue became real his confidence failed and he withdrew. This created a sense of failure and frustration. When it was recognised that W's desire was serious he was supported by myself, establishing a relationship with W over a period, giving confidence in the support he would receive if and when he moved. This gave him the space to make a final decision to move out of residential care. The support he received was intensive at first from both myself and his previous residential care staff on an outreach basis. As his confidence grew the support diminished as he established himself in his flat.

* * *

The changes which have recently taken place for W clearly have a lot to do with her treatment in hospital and subsequent long-term medication. The relationships which she has had with her support workers, however, have also played a significant part in her success in her re-establishment in her flat. In the recognition of a `masked' mental health condition, work by the support team was crucial in its early diagnosis. Subsequent support in her hospitalisation and a late period in hospital, following an accident, were vital in allowing her to continue her more successful tenancy.

* * *

The main factor to bring about the change in M's life has got to be living with less people in a homely environment and a care team with more time to talk her and listen. M needs motivating and encouraging to do everything, was often called lazy by the other clients, but it was just how she was. I have to admit, M did not stand when she could sit, even to push the hoover. M would sit on anything, she has been know to sit on a raised flowerbed and nearly on a baby in a pushchair, but not quite thank goodness! The confidence she gained again came from the people around her being able to give her time to let her do things. When she did do something such as making a cup of tea (with supervision) this was an achievement for M and she was pleased as punch. M loves animals and there is a cat in the house who M used to talk a lot to, even to tell him off, which again helped with her speech. Most people who knew M had to love her and she was sadly missed by all when she had to move into the nursing home.

* * *

Some of the factors bringing about this change are the support and encouragement she gets from the care team who encourage her to act independently, to speak up and give opinions which are listened to and valued. She makes choices in shopping, food clothes, buying furnishings and anything of importance in her everyday life. All of these have brought about a dramatic change in the way she sees herself.

★ ★ ★

I believe the following factors have contributed to bringing about these changes for Mr S: (1) He has opportunities to make informed choices as to what is purchased. This is because he can see the range of goods available by going to supermarkets, shops, pubs, restaurants, clothes shops, hair stylists etc. (2) By having the opportunity to support his speech by gestures, e.g. pointing, his communication has become much more effective and purposeful. This is less frustrating or humiliating to him, and so his confidence to try out new words and phrases have increased. (3) As he now lives in a much smaller group, Mr S no longer has to compete for staff attention. Hence staff can take the time to listen to what he is saying, without his having to shout or give up trying before being understood. (4) Mr S is treated with warmth, kindness and respect by the staff team, the home's philosophy being one which focuses on his ability rather than disability.

★ ★ ★

Living in a normal sort of house in a normal road. Living with only a small number of people, living somewhere where staff are able to give you time, time to understand your needs, time to provide those needs. Having people work with you that treat you as an individual and let you decide about things affecting your life. Having people work with you that can take you out on your own, and help to choose your own clothes. The staff encouraged him to speak up for himself and helped/ encouraged him to be more independent. No one shouts at him or tells him he will do this or will not do that. The change in this gentleman has been tremendous, and can be attributed to many small things. I am positive that some of the main factors are being treated as an individual and having self respect and know that you have a voice, and learning that you are you and that matters.

★ ★ ★

1. TV not switched on all day; much better ratio of staff to clients; more time to 'get-to-know' the person; more interesting things to do and see outside; less competition from other clients for attention; more relaxed and informal environment.

2. Loss of freedom; loss of choice; loss of available space; small restricted environment.

★ ★ ★

Feeling secure after getting used to the community he lives in, calling the house, 'home', choice being able to choose his own clothes, toiletries, food etc. Being treated as an individual with respect, having his opinions listened to and acted upon; living in a small group home with people he likes and trusts. Being encouraged to communicate his needs have all been possible factors in changing this gentlemen into a happy, healthy, socially acceptable individual who is loved by all who meet him.

* * *

1. Smaller client groups – clients get more individual attention.
2. Smaller and more pleasant living environment.
3. A large garden where Mr G can walk in safety.
4. Regular personal plan meetings.
5. Having privacy of his own room.
6. Living area is smaller therefore staff are still with clients even when busy.
7. House routine geared to clients' needs rather than other departments as in hospitals, e.g. mealtimes more relaxed because we aren't working to the caterer's timetable.

* * *

Probably the staff:client ratio which has obviously increased. Staff have been able to spend more quality time with D to help him to develop his skills and learn new ones. Because we have access to community services, D has been able to meet more people and to interact with them appropriately.

* * *

More staffing.
Living with less people.
Better finances.
Own room and personal possessions.
Decrease in challenging behaviours due to the programmes of care which are consistently carried out and regularly evaluated and updated.
Transport.
Homely environment.
Family environment.

* * *

It's easy enough to close down a hospital and move people to the community – just a case of logistics – but what then?
One of the factors that helped 'our move' to be a success and to continue to be so was the simultaneous development of a day service for clients

which was operational prior to clients moving to their new homes. We also spent a lot of time on staff training and staff/client orientation to their new neighbourhoods and a new way of life.

Other factors include:

- a clear recognition of the purpose of the service
- a willingness by staff to learn new skills and new approaches to people, e.g. gentle teaching
- a supportive management structure and organisational philosophy which put the client at the centre of all things
- a good staff support network (working in the community can be very stressful at times)
- a recognition that sometimes people need to take risks in order to develop.

★ ★ ★

Moving away from the dehumanising practices of long-stay hospitals.
Moving to a new home/which he shares with two other people.
His own space/bedroom/living areas.
His own furniture/clothes/music centre/tapes/CDs/photographs.
Regular holidays with a one-to-one support.
His own key worker/associate worker.
Structured care plans/ based on ordinary life principles.
Regaining contact with his family.
Making other friends within the community.
Using general services/GP/dentist/college.
Structured weekly leisure activities/day services.
The opportunity to make choices.
Being respected and valued with the people he lives with and the staff that support him.
Gaining a regular income/ through benefits – allowing him to save/ and spend on items he wishes to buy/ or on nights out.

★ ★ ★

There are many significant factors, several that I have already mentioned overleaf. Smaller staff:resident ratios allow for more time and more consideration in the individuals needs and development. Whereas in large institutional living, staff ratios were the opposite, personal time could not be spent supporting these factors. As mentioned before, increased personal autonomy is an extremely important factor, giving individuals the right to make choices for themselves. Regular IPP meetings between D and staff allows him to take active decisions over issues to experience. The position of the living environment is also important, instead of being situated 'out of town' as most large, self-contained institutions usually were, living in a home, which consists of smaller group occupancy and is situated in a 'normal' residential area, allows D and other residents alike to use local facilities, which in turn integrates individuals into the community – making them feel more valued members of that community.

★ ★ ★

- Moving out of hospital (positive)
- being close enough to get to know others – residents and staff (positive)
- only being able to be with carers/residents (if unable to go out unaccompanied) (negative).

★ ★ ★

Increased staff:resident ratios.

Physical location – nearer to family and community facilities.

Access to benefits system Home manager has more opportunity to plan for residents needs on an individual basis due to reduced client group size.

Access to GP service enables easier access to specialist medical treatment.

★ ★ ★

I feel that more personal attention from staff may have helped S gain in confidence so that she is now willing to take part in occupational and social activities. There is now more staff per client ratio than when S lived in hospital. In recent years more finance has been made available to help people with learning disabilities move out of large institutions into smaller premises in the community. S's new house was purpose built with more homely and modern facilities than her old home.

★ ★ ★

1. The new group home is situated in such a way that this lady does not have any major roads to cross until she reaches town, where she is then able to use designated crossing areas.
2. The lady has a newfound confidence due to: (a) an improvement in health, i.e. epilepsy better controlled which has virtually eliminated seizures; (b) as her independence grew she felt able to attempt new skills.

★ ★ ★

Staff teams, working with St Anne's Philosophy (Aims and Values) promote freedom of choice and nurture individual growth and development. Small group homes lead to relaxation of routines. Residents involved in all aspects of daily living. In this 'normal environment' residents grow in confidence and acquire new skills, both personal and social; this then leads to integration within local communities.

* * *

Society as a whole has changed. People with LD are now treated as human beings with rights. People working with LD have fought for these changes but it has taken a long time to come round. People realised that small houses in the community were easier to manage and better for residents that the old institutions, but it was a money issue. It was cheaper to house twenty-three in one villa with three staff, than have four or five houses with three staff in each. I think the changes have been brought about by people who work with LD and who push for better services for these people. I also think it still has a fair way to go and even more improvements can be made, but again money is the key issue.

* * *

He is now living in a smaller group, with a higher staff ratio. He receives more attention on a 1:1 basis. The other residents communicate with him, as well as the carers. He has more interactive liaising within the local community, and contact with his neighbours. He now lives in a more homely environment, with more personal belongings. He attends more appropriate activities, and makes more choices on a daily basis.

* * *

The above extracts from questionnaires indicate the sorts of factors staff believe to be crucial in improving quality of life: focus upon individual needs, consideration for individual requests, aspirations, respect and giving dignity, enabling privacy, improving contacts and relationships with the world outside and helping individuals to communicate. These areas of activity form the heart of social care in the community, but have never been given formal recognition in the sense of being used as yardstick in national inquiries on residential services. When considering the function of community homes, observers and researchers choose to use blanket statements like 'improving quality of life', 'integrating people in community activities', 'providing respite to relatives' or 'dealing with the transition from hospital', rarely assessing and analysing what these goals mean in practice. This may relate to why professionalisation and training of residential staff has not been high on any political agenda. (The Jay Committee Report almost two decades ago was the last to consider this problem in learning disabilities, but this was largely a function of the political mood of the time which tended to favour a rational social planning approach.)

Consistent with findings from a recent national review on aims and outcomes of residential services (Emerson *et al.*, 1996) the stated achievements in quality of life of individual residents were: participation, social indicators, choice, competence, community presence.

POSITIVE CHANGES

- E More one-to-one contact, an IP system, more staff attention.
- E More privacy (own bedrooms); personal pride in room, furnishing and equipment, personal possessions.
- E Increased choice (food, music, when come in/go to bed, family contacts, clothes, holidays, how long to spend in the bath, purchase own furniture, more consultation).
- E Skill development (better speech, fewer bad/disruptive behaviours, obsessions, less biting/nipping; self help, e.g. feeding, table manners improved).
- E Sense of contentment (less abuse from others, fear).
- E More freedom, independence (expression of individuality, financial independence).
- E More involvement with 'community' (access to public facilities, transport, libraries parks, regular outings, GP services, discos/parties, using local transport, taxis, meals out, walks, visits).
- E More sociable, confident (pleasant to be with, more self assured, less solitary, good personal relationships with staff).

NEGATIVE CHANGES

- E Restricted to a 'smaller' environment.

One conclusion from this admittedly selective trawl of examples is that changes noted were *almost all positive*. An example of change in the negative direction concerned level of restriction to which residents were subjected, referring to the contrast with the ability to 'roam freely around large grounds [in hospital] visiting various areas, departments and individuals' as one staff member put it.

A second point was that changes seemed to be based on descriptions, impressions or vignettes (word-pictures) of clients' lives, no reference to structured assessments or measured changes. This discloses perhaps an important distinction between current functions of health service as opposed to social service or independent sector care. The former is tending to deploy ordinary housing to assess clients' abilities and so on and then moving them on to more homelike environments where formal monitoring seems to occur less frequently. There is an argument where this would be regarded as damaging. Not only do discontinuities in frontline service provision frequently disrupt individual programmes and the personal relationships between staff and users, but to dispense with structured individual programme planning fails to provide evidence of achievement. As stated earlier, the descriptions perceptibly failed to incorporate a client/user perspective.

Overview

> Quality of life values are applicable at every level in society – from the individual and family to national and international levels. *They provide criteria for discerning what is acceptable and unacceptable with reference to a set of standards.* These standard apply equally to individual and to corporate behaviour. Quality of life values challenge the behaviour of all kinds of corporate bodies and social institutions, including multinational companies, political institutions, the church, professional groups and voluntary associations. (Seed and Lloyd, 1997, p.207)

A central purpose of this paper is to place community residential care in a policy and professional context. It was in the early 1980s that housing was first recognised as an adjunct of community care and that housing developments needed to operate alongside developments in health and social services. The Personal Social Services Research Unit at Kent, in its studies on deinstitutionalisation (1985), observed that 'the true capital cost of care in the community has not been recognised', pointing to the need for funds to be made available both to convert existing housing stock and to put up new buildings where necessary.

A search conducted during 1981 of existing housing schemes[1] for people with learning disabilities or with mental health problems revealed a total of 1048 schemes throughout England and Wales (Ritchie, Keegan and Bosanquet, 1983). Of these 662 (63%) were people for mental health problems, 355 (34%) were for those with learning disabilities, and 31 (3%) were intended for both groups. Approximately two-thirds (65%) of the provision was based in housing department properties, 28 per cent in housing association properties and 6 per cent in properties belonging to voluntary organisations. This balance has now clearly shifted, with housing associations and trusts providing the bulk of homes. Around this period several research studies were conducted on housing-based models of care, covering support methods, community networks and living arrangements (Malin, 1983; Atkinson, 1985; Flynn, 1985). Summarising literature in an official (then) DHSS review McKnight (1981) listed the following (mainly research) findings which can be summarised as:

> the size of living unit is more important than the size of facility, small living units being associated with a higher quality of care; an enriched environment has positive effects on resident development compared to an impoverished environment; there are indications that unit location in a catchment area with good transport facilities is favourable. Staff training background is not seen as a significant factor in care but the numbers of trained staff are low; decentralisation, less rigid rules and the involvement of staff at all levels may improve care; there is a need for more communication among staff and the development of a clear, shared policy; the need for separate unit based staff accommodation has been questioned; residential staff lack support from outside professionals. There is hardly any evidence on the appropriate ability, sex and age mix of residents. Community attitudes are important in the setting up and continuing success of a community residence, initial resistance coming from a minority of the local community; understanding of mental handicap is related to opinion of and opposition to a residence; opposition diminishes and acceptance increases with contact as the home is in operation.

---

[1] A scheme was defined as a unit or set of units based within one building, offering housing accommodation; the term should not suggest a specialised form of accommodation since in most cases it involved ordinary housing.

It is in the context of the NHS and Community Care Act 1990 and with the opening up of the internal market in health/social care that the range of provision has diversified, with less government-supported research, more fragmentation and private sector involvement in residential services. Simons (1997) claims that in the UK the absence of any ideological commitment or policy direction from central government has resulted in a largely pragmatic approach to development of residential services for people with learning disabilities. This has inevitably influenced the way in which units are being staffed: the pattern of training, for example, has not been consistent.

Wood, Berry and Cowell (1985) identified three key areas for staff training: dealing with inappropriate behaviour, engaging residents in activities and precision-teaching techniques. Similarly, Knapp, Cambridge and Thomason (1989) reported that the training and skills most highly valued by managers were those concerned with dealing with challenging behaviour, assessment techniques and communication skills. In addition to skills-based training, it is also recognised that values-based training plays a critical role in the development of effective staff (Rose and Holmes, 1991; Harper, 1994). In addition to training, Allen, Pahl and Quine (1990) and Kroese and Fleming (1992) stress the importance of staff support and supervision together with the maintenance of organisational morale. Sharrard (1992) concludes that the major issues of concern for residential staff are linked to work-related stress arising from 'personnel problems' rather than user-related issues. Sharrard stresses that before normalised and positive outcomes can be realised for users, personnel issues such as pay, promotion and career structure, rosters, staff ratios and so on need to be addressed.

Whereas the data from the St Anne's questionnaires paint a fairly rosy picture of staff 'coping' and an implied consistency between methods adopted and attainments in users' quality of life, other studies demonstrate significant staff training needs. McVilly's (1997) work shows a sizeable disparity between the mean importance of various training areas to workers and the workers' perceptions of the degree to which they had been prepared to undertake the tasks in question. Respondents attached a high degree of importance to skills such as dealing with challenging and inappropriate behaviour, assessment techniques, skills teaching, communication strategies, engaging and fostering tenant participation in daily activities and assisting tenants to make choices.

Other studies have shown the ambivalence of using values-based training (or Social Role Valorisation (SRV)) (Lavender, 1985; Beyer and Scally, 1992; Harper, 1994) when it is not accompanied by instruction in how values are to be transformed into daily practices relating to individual clients or by instruction on the function of staff attitudes in shaping ability, prior to the instruction of any 'philosophy of service provision'. McVilly's study (1997) states that the issue of concern most frequently cited by respondents was the size of the organisation and that it had grown too large, making residential staff feel isolated from the decision-making process.

Furthermore, current research has supported the rather negative picture of staff isolation, both professionally and practically, with evidence of failures of the individual client planning approach (Simons, Booth, and Booth, 1990) and the general disregard for what staff actually do in their role as careworkers (Felce, 1996; Mansell, 1994). The authors attribute success of the earlier, 1980s' demonstration projects to the 'active support' model adopted. They argue that as emphasis was placed on ensuring that staff knew what they were meant to do and how to do it, the main focus of activity was directed towards their engagement with the people with learning disabilities. This has been much rarer in the second generation models of housing that have been the subject of formal evaluations. Both Mansell and Felce point to failure of management in services to monitor the outcomes for people with learning disabilities, suggesting that the quality of many services are not judged by what they achieve. Indeed, Mansell argues that in many instances the managers of services are not interested in quality issues, being much more concerned with costs.

This chapter has attempted to trace some of the major strands of community care policy and consider 'quality of life' as a viable aim of residential services. This aim is however a fuzzy one; the purpose and plan of residential projects are not always articulated and the role of staff not spelled out. A forward move would be to place individual user plans as a top priority and to resolve the policy objective; what are the functions of community residential units and what part do they play in an overall scheme?

The training and responsibilities of staff need re-examination and review. As more emphasis is now placed on providing independent living arrangements and residential care in housing than it was 20 years ago, many more people's needs are being met in this way – the figures show that. Yet the area has become almost invisible, nationally at any rate, of in-depth data on how such units are run, their achievements and difficulties, how users experience living there and what part this type of provision plays in local planning. This is not the place to explore such a suggestion, but until this matter is reviewed at national level then there can be no assurances on standards, how users are treated, and the main risk and professional issues involved.

References

Allen, P., Pahl, J. and Quine, L. (1990) *Care Staff in Transition.* London: HMSO.

Atkinson, D. (1985) 'The use of participant observation and respondent diaries in a study of ordinary living.' *British Journal of Mental Subnormality XXXI, I, 60, 33–46.*

Atkinson, D. and Williams, F. (1990) *Know Me as I Am – An Anthology of Poetry, Prose and Art from People with Learning Disabilities.* London: Hodder and Stoughton.

Beyer, S. and Scally, M. (1992) 'Integrating staff and service development: lessons from West Glamorgan.' *Clinical Psychology Forum 45,* 2–9.

Bright, L. (1997) *Harm's Way.* London: Counsel and Care.

Dalley, G. (1992) 'Social welfare ideologies and normalisation.' In H. Brown and H. Smith (eds) *Normalisation: A Reader for the Nineties.* London: Routledge.

Department of Health (1989) *Caring for People: Community Care in the Next Decade and Beyond.* Cm 849. London: HMSO.

Department of Health (1990) *Community Care in the Next Decade and Beyond Policy Guidance.* London: HMSO.

DHSS (1971) *Better Services for the Mentally Handicapped.* Cmnd 4683. London: HMSO.

Emerson, E. (1985) 'Evaluating the impact of deinstitutionalisation on the lives of mentally retarded people.' *American Journal of Mental Deficiency 90,* 277–88.

Emerson, E., Mansell, J. and McGill, P. (1994) *Severe Learning Disabilities and Challenging Behaviours: Designing High Quality Services.* London: Chapman and Hall.

Emerson, E., Cullen, C., Hatton, C. and Cross, B. (1996) *Residential Provision for People with Learning Disabilities: Summary Report.* Manchester: HARC, University of Manchester.

Felce, D. (1996) 'Quality of support for ordinary living.' In J. Mansell and K. Ericsson (eds) *Deinstitutionalisation and Community Living: Intellectual Disability Services in Britain, Scandinavia and the USA.* London: Chapman and Hall.

Felce, D. and Perry, J. (1993) *Quality of Life: A Contribution to its Definition and Measurement.* Cardiff: Mental handicap in Wales, Applied Research Unit.

Flynn, M. (1995) 'Objectives and prognoses recorded in the case records of mentally handicapped adults living in their own homes.' *British Journal of Social Work 15,* 519–42.

Fox, N. (1993) *Postmodernism, Sociology and Health.* Buckingham: Open University Press.

Glennerster, H. and Lewis, J. (1996) *Implementing the New Community Care.* Buckingham: Open University Press.

Goffman, E. (1961) *Asylums: Essays on the Social Situation of Mental Patients and other Inmates.* New York: Anchor Books.

Graham, H. (1983) 'Caring: a labour of love.' In J. Finch and D. Groves (eds) *A Labour of Love: Women, Work and Caring.* London: Routledge.

Griffiths Report (1988) *Community Care: An Agenda for Action.* London: HMSO.

Harper, G. (1994) 'Evaluating a training package for staff working with people with learning disabilities prior to hospital closure.' *British Journal of Developmental Disabilities 40*, 1, 45–53.

Jay Committee (1979) *Report of the Committee of Enquiry into Mental Handicap Nursing and Care,* Volume 1. Cmnd. 7468. London: HMSO.

Knapp, M., Cambridge, P. and Thomason, C. (1989) *Final Report of the Evaluation of the Care in the Community Initiative.* Canterbury: PSSRU, University of Kent.

Kroese, B. and Fleming, I. (1992) 'Staff's attitudes and working conditions in community-based group homes of people with mental handicaps.' *Mental Handicap Research 5*, 1, 82–91.

Lavender, A. (1985) 'Quality of care and staff practices in long-stay settings.' In F. Watts (ed) *New Developments in Clinical Psychology.* London: Wiley.

Liu, B.C. (1976) *Quality of Life Indicators in US Metropolitan Areas: A Statistical Analysis.* New York: Praeger Publishers.

Malin, N. (1978) *Staff Attitudes in Mental Handicap.* (Scottish Society for the Mentally Handicapped.) Glasgow: Bell and Bain.

Malin, N. (1983) *Group Homes for Mentally Handicapped People.* London: HMSO.

Mansell, J. (1994) *Severe Learning Disabilities and Challenging Behaviours.* London: Chapman and Hall.

Mansell, J. and Ericsson, K. (1996) *Deinstitutionalisation and Community Living.* London: Chapman and Hall.

Manthorpe, J. (1994) 'The family and informal care.' In N. Malin (ed) *Implementing Community Care.* Buckingham: Open University Press.

McKnight, D. (1981) *Review of Literature on Non-Institutional Care.* London: HMSO.

McVilly, K. (1997) 'Residential staff: how they view their training and professional support.' *British Journal of Learning Disabilities 25*, 13–20.

Michalos, A. (1976) 'Measuring the quality of life.' In W.R. Shea and J. King-Farlow (eds) *Values and the Quality of Life.* New York: Science History Publications.

PSSRU (1985) *Care in the Community: Housing and Support Services.* Canterbury: The University of Kent.

Ritchie, J., Keegan, J. and Bosanquet, N. (1983) *Housing for Mentally Ill and Mentally Handicapped People.* London: HMSO.

Rose, J. and Holmes, S. (1991) 'Changing staff attitudes to the sexuality of people with mental handicaps: an evaluative comparison of one and three day workshops.' *Mental Handicap Research 4*, 67–79.

Seebohm Report (1968) *Report of the Committee on Local Authority and Allied Personal Social Services.* Cmnd 3703. London: HMSO.

Seed, P. and Lloyd, G. (1997) *Quality of Life.* London: Jessica Kingsley Publishers.

Sharrard, H. (1992) 'Feeling the strain: job stress and satisfaction of direct care staff in the mental handicap service.' *British Journal of Mental Subnormality 38*, 1, 32–8.

Simons, K., Booth, T. and Booth, W. (1990) *Outward Bound: Relocation and Community Care for People with Learning Difficulties.* Milton Keynes: Open University Press.

Simons, K. (1997) 'Residential care, or housing and support?' *British Journal of Learning Disabilities 25*, 1–7.

Sinson, J.C. (1993) *Group Homes and Community Integration of Developmentally Disabled People: Microinstitutionalism.* London: Jessica Kingsley Publishers.

Thomason, C. (1985) *Care in the Community: Housing and Support Services.* Canterbury: PSSRU, University of Kent.

Ungerson, C. (1997) 'Give them the money: is cash a route to empowerment?' *Social Policy and Administration 31*, 1 March, 45–53.

Walmsley, J. (1993) 'Talking to top people: some issues relating to citizenship of people with learning disabilities.' In J. Swain, V. Finkelstein, J. French and M. Oliver (eds) *Disabling Barriers – Enabling Environments.* Buckingham: Open University Press/Sage.

Williams, F. (1992) 'The family: change, challenge and contradiction.' In *Social Welfare and Social Work Yearbook 1992.* Buckingham: Open University Press.

Wolfensberger, W. (1972) *The Principle of Normalisation in Human Services.* Toronto: National Institute of Mental Retardation.

Wood, J., Berry, I. and Cowell, B. (1985) 'Training staff in a large residential setting for people with mental handicaps.' *Mental Handicap 13*, 97–9.

CHAPTER 5

The Resettlement of Single Homeless People

What Works and for Whom?

Alan Deacon

One of the most striking features of services for single homeless people in recent years has been the importance attached to resettlement work. This is true of both government policies such as the closure of the former Department of Social Security resettlement units and of developments within the voluntary sector such as the Open House programme coordinated by Crisis. The objective is no longer to just provide accommodation but to encourage and facilitate resettlement.

This, of course, raises the question as to what constitutes effective resettlement? What forms of accommodation should those being resettled be expected to move to? What kinds of support would they need to be able to cope in that accommodation? How long would they have to remain there for it to be judged a success? What criteria could be used to judge if those who have been resettled are indeed leading happier and more fulfilled lives?

The debate around such questions is an extremely important one in two respects. In policy terms, it is clearly essential that provision meets the accommodation and support needs of homeless people if the outcome is not to be demoralising and damaging for those affected and a waste of resources. More fundamentally, however, to ask what someone needs in order to be resettled is in effect to ask why he or she became homeless in the first place, and why he or she has remained homeless despite the existing provision. This means, therefore, that arguments about resettlement reflect a much broader debate about the nature of single homelessness and about the relative importance of individual and structural factors in explaining the growth of the problem. If homelessness is primarily caused by personal factors, then the key to resettlement is to change the way people behave. This might mean helping them to escape from a dependency on alcohol or other drugs, to abandon a transient lifestyle or petty crime, or to make a more active search for work. Alternatively, if homelessness is rooted in poverty and a shortage of suitable accommodation, then resettlement requires first and foremost access to such accommodation, advice on social security and other benefits, and possibly some help with domestic skills for those who have been forced to live in hostels for long periods.

In practice, of course, these two explanations are not mutually exclusive. As the American writer Christopher Jencks has argued in trying to explain homelessness, 'we need to replace our instinctive either-or approach to blame with a both-and approach' (Jencks, 1994, p.48). Nevertheless, the question of balance remains crucial and it will be seen below that different policy prescriptions reflect contrasting perceptions of the causes of homelessness.

This chapter, then, attempts to provide two things. First, a broad overview of the debate about the nature of resettlement and how it might best be achieved for different groups of single homeless people. Second, a brief account of the closure of the former DSS resettlement units. The latter is a crucial development in which St Anne's has played an important role.

The resettlement debate

Changing attitudes towards the single homeless

The current debate as to the nature of resettlement has its origins in the late 1970s. Specifically it arose out of two interrelated factors. The first was a growing recognition of the increasing size and diversity of the single homeless population. The second was the evidence which was emerging about the appalling conditions which were being experienced by the residents of some large hostels.

The problem of vagrancy had, of course, been an enduring preoccupation of the poor law in the nineteenth and early twentieth centuries, and, as Crowther noted, the casual poor had always been 'one rung below the able bodied settled poor' (Crowther, 1981, p.247). During the interwar period vagrancy was still viewed as a symptom of personal inadequacy, although this came to be presented less as an unwillingness to work than as an inability to do so (Krafchik, 1983, p.196). Even in the 1960s it was widely assumed that the single homeless conformed to the stereotype of the 'down and out', and this appeared to be borne out by studies of those resident in large hostels or in what were then called reception centres (National Assistance Board, 1966; Crossley and Denmark, 1969). This emphasis upon personal explanations of homelessness was also to be found in the voluntary sector, and Watson and Austerberry have documented the preoccupation of many voluntary agencies with the deviant nature and 'welfare' needs of the single homeless (Watson and Austerberry 1986, pp.56–9).

The change in attitudes which seems to have occurred in the late 1970s did not follow a specific refutation of the earlier studies but reflected a belief that they only told part of the story. It was argued that although some homeless people may well exhibit behavioural problems they were a minority, and, moreover, they were becoming a smaller and smaller minority as the numbers of single homeless people grew inexorably. As the authors of the influential study *Single and Homeless* noted:

> It came to be recognised that the problem incorporated wider numbers and a greater range of needs reflecting not just individual problems ... This changing perspective did not deny that ... within the single homeless population there are disproportionate numbers of people with a range of personal difficulties. However it did suggest that single homelessness should not be seen solely in terms of people with problems, and that the remedy for many of the homeless lay in access to housing rather than social services. (Drake, O'Brien, and Biebuyck, 1981, pp.9–10)

The causes of the growth in single homelessness are complex and beyond the scope of this chapter. The important point here, however, is that what are seen as the most important factors are predominately structural. They include the reduction in the amount of accommodation available to rent, the increased incidence of relationship breakdown, the persistence of long-term unemployment, the closure of large mental institutions and the decline in the relative value of social security benefits, especially those paid to single people under 25. Few would argue that single homelessness has increased because of changes in behaviour, whilst recent research has demonstrated still further the scale of the problem and the diversity of those affected by it (Anderson, Kemp and Quilgars, 1993; Anderson, 1994).

This change in the perceptions of single homeless people held by both policy makers and practitioners was reinforced by a growing awareness of the unsuitability and inadequacy of much of the existing provision. In particular the problems of large hostels were extensively documented. They were too large and too impersonal, often of a forbidding appearance and with a poor reputation in the local area. Residents enjoyed scant privacy and had little freedom to decide when and what to eat, when and what to watch on the television. Moreover, such hostels created the problem they were supposed to solve. Residents were not required to shop, to cook, or to perform a myriad of other tasks, and so they became progressively 'deskilled' and less and less able to cope with life outside a hostel. The argument was later restated by David Donnison: 'By confining people to institutional life, and so preventing them from learning housekeeping skills, hostels create a permanent demand for their own services' (Donnison, 1991, p.14).

More fundamentally the lack of security of tenure and exposure to other residents meant that large hostels all but imposed a transient lifestyle upon many of their residents, only for that lifestyle to be then cited as evidence of an individual pathology which required and justified the retention of such hostels. Once trapped in the 'circuit of homelessness', it became increasingly difficult to secure access to mainstream housing. This point was made very forcefully in one of many reports on large hostels produced in the early 1980s:

> Once a single man or woman becomes homeless the chances are that s/he will remain so. The limited options available to homeless people to alter their circumstances do not transcend their homelessness but merely alter, usually marginally, the conditions under which they endure it. Once a single man or woman becomes homeless the chances are that s/he will remain so. This forced unsettledness then becomes, in popular concepts a personal characteristic, used to justify the continuation of those institutions which provide temporary and insecure acc-ommodation. (Lewisham Single Housing Group, 1981, p.14)

The 'good housekeeping' model

The above quotation is, of course, a very clear presentation of a structural explanation of why people become and remain homeless. Moreover, the implications for policy are equally clear – many of those living in hostels would prefer to live independently in houses and flats and would be able to do so if given appropriate preparation and support. Indeed, the report *Single and Homeless* quoted earlier argued that only 'a small minority' of single homeless people would 'need a fully-staffed hostel'. Instead less than two-thirds would require 'little more than sensitive housing management' and a further third 'would need a minimal support regime.' (Drake *et al.*,

1982, pp.9–10). These recommendations were particularly influential because they were produced by a study which had been funded by the Department of the Environment. Furthermore, they appeared to be confirmed by the success of resettlement schemes in Manchester and Glasgow which had made extensive use of homemakers in resettling people in local authority houses and flats (Dant and Deacon, 1989, pp. 7–10). The outcome was the emergence of a new consensus which replaced the former emphasis upon individual pathology with what has been termed the 'good housekeeping' model of resettlement. This new consensus rested upon a number of assumptions:

E that hostels were inherently damaging to those who lived in them, but

E that this damage was unnecessary since many residents would prefer to live independently and were quite capable of doing so, but

E that in order to cope with independent living many hostel dwellers would need instruction in household skills, and some measure of personal and social support in the period following the move.

It is, of course, all too easy to exaggerate the extent of any apparent consensus and it should be recognised that Madeline Drake, one of the authors of the *Single and Homeless* report, told a Housing Centre Trust seminar in January 1985 that 'it may be that some people need communal living' and that at a time of housing cuts it was questionable 'whether there is no further need for big hostels' (Drake, 1985, p.96). Nonetheless it remains true that there was a widespread assumption that large hostels were discredited, and that effective resettlement meant training people to live independently in mainstream housing. This was the conclusion drawn by CHAR – the most important pressure group for the single homeless – which insisted that 'ordinary independent housing' should be 'the major element' of any rehousing scheme (CHAR, 1983, p.19). Similarly, Chris Holmes argued that the *Single and Homeless* report provided 'the most authoritative repudiation' of the idea that hostel residents would not be able to cope with a home of their own (Holmes, 1986, p.204).

The experience of the Camberwell Replacement Scheme
In subsequent years the 'good housekeeping' model has been questioned and challenged on a number of grounds and from a range of viewpoints. The first important source of evidence as to what worked and what did not work in

resettlement came from the experience of the Camberwell Replacement Scheme (CRS) in London.

The unit, in Camberwell, South London, was by far the largest and most controversial of the resettlement units. Indeed, the publicity given to events in Camberwell did much to damage the image and reputation of the units in general (Deacon and Jones, 1988, p.171). The replacement scheme was announced in November 1981, although Camberwell itself did not close until September 1985. The scheme had several components, including the direct placement of some Camberwell residents in local authority housing by a Joint Assessment and Resettlement Team (JART) (GLC, 1985; Duncan and Downey, 1985) and the provision of a total of 130 direct-access beds by four local authorities. The greater part of CRS, however, consisted of 855 bed spaces in small housing units, developed by housing associations and managed by voluntary organisations. Of these, 100 bed spaces were designated as high care and the remaining 755 as low/medium care. All, however, were in so-called second stage accommodation – the funding did not provide for follow up support to residents who were moved on to other accommodation. An important point is that in the great majority of cases CRS monies constituted a further source of funding to organisations and agencies which were already active in the field. CRS enabled these agencies to grow and to develop, but it did not create them nor necessarily change their way of working. As a result, CRS came to encompass a diversity of approaches and a wide range of provision.

This was particularly true of the stance adopted towards resettlement work. Tilt and Denford (1986) examined the work of 16 projects and identified four broad approaches which they saw as constituting a continuum from most assertive to passive. The first they labelled 'training/ resocialisation'. This was characterised by the provision of regular and compulsory training in household skills. Move-on accommodation was guaranteed and the move had to be completed within a specified period. The second approach – 'assertive and interventionistic' – was similarly based upon the 'good housekeeping' model. Residents were required to move through and out of the project, and there was regular and intensive contact with staff to achieve this end. In contrast, the third approach – 'resident determined' – was marked by an expectation of move-on in the longer term but no pressure was put upon residents in the early months of their stay, and the pace of any preparation programme was effectively decided by the residents. Finally, there was a fourth and most passive approach, which Tilt and Denford described as 'come and live with us and we'll see'. Here the hostel effectively served as a sanctuary for the most vulnerable, and the transfer to the project was itself viewed as an act of 'resettlement' (Tilt and Denford 1986, pp.30–1).

It followed from this that although each project stated that its objective was the resettlement of residents, there was no agreement as to what represented success or failure in resettlement work.

> The projects were roughly divided into those working to achieve rehabilitation and residents' return to a more normal lifestyle, and those where an improvement in the quality of life and greater happiness in whichever location, were seen as more important than necessarily achieving total normalisation. (p.37)

Despite this diversity of approaches to resettlement on the ground, Tilt and Denford went on to present a two-stage model of the process. First comes resettlement within the hostel. This requires the stabilisation of the individual's lifestyle and the acquisition of new skills and attitudes. The second stage is the transfer to more independent accommodation – move-on.

> Move-on must surely be the acid test of effective resettlement, because it is only in the new environment that the new skills, knowledge and attitudes can really be tested. (p.56)

To be sure, move-on did not necessarily mean a house or flat. Recent 'developments in resettlement thinking' had led to 'the refinement of the concept' and a move away from

> the old ideal of putting residents through a resettlement mill so that they could graduate to a home of their own. Many residents would never cope independently and what was needed for them was a good supply of permanent shared housing or at the very least sheltered accommodation. (p.53)

Even so, the pattern remained one of personal preparation and training, followed by a transfer to somewhere more independent.

Such transfers, however, proved to be the most significant weakness of the CRS projects, because of the difficulty of providing any support for people who had moved on in the absence of specific funding for such follow up work. 'Without exception staff agonised about this point … to many … all but negated the attempt they had already made to resettle a resident' (p.43). In general, projects had 'developed a hotchpotch of informal make-do solutions to support their ex-residents' (p.44), including home visits, invitations to ex-residents to visit the project at specified times, and referral to community-based organisations.

To some extent, of course, the issue of follow-up was a problem of success, since it presupposed that the agency had been able to secure suitable accommodation for their residents. Tilt and Denford noted that this became progressively more difficult the longer the projects had been open. The well-recognised consequence is the 'silting up' of hostels as more and more beds are occupied by people who do not need the support of the hostel, but for whom no alternative accommodation is available (p.42). This problem is, of course, common to all resettlement schemes. Indeed the report of a study of 25 hostels in five local authority areas emphasised how perspectives of what constituted resettlement were influenced by the resources available. The lack of alternative housing led staff to focus more and more on the improvement of life within the hostel: 'Because it is so difficult to find accommodation, staff concentrate on more achievable objects and these "domestic priorities" are inevitably reinforced' (Garside, Grimshaw and Ward, 1990, p.92).

The experience of the Leeds Shaftesbury Project

An alternative view of the resettlement process was presented by Dant and Deacon, who drew upon the findings of their study of the Leeds Shaftesbury Project (LSP). This project offered intensive help and support to people moving from large hostels in Leeds to independent houses and flats. Dant and Deacon concluded that there was no single factor or combination of factors which determined 'success or failure' in such rehousing, although it was clear that people were more likely to 'settle down' after leaving a hostel if they had already been living in the Leeds area for some time. This suggested that the success of the rehousing scheme in Glasgow reflected 'to some degree the local and stable nature of the single homeless population of that city' (Dant and Deacon, 1989, p.100).

More fundamentally, however, Dant and Deacon argued that resettlement was not simply a matter of rehousing but involved the establishment and maintenance of a 'home'. The notion of a home 'was not tied to any particular unit of accommodation' (p.68). Indeed, it was often more difficult to establish a home in properties designed for a nuclear family – the very thing which some single homeless people were seeking to escape from. Dant and Deacon described a home as a place which had three broad qualities:

E it offered appropriate and adequate shelter and some security of tenure

E it contained the equipment and furniture necessary for the performance of normal domestic tasks

E it was sufficiently comfortable and attractive to the individual for him or her 'to feel at ease in it, attracted to it, to identify it as their home and invite others on that basis' (p.68).

The difference between resettlement and rehousing, then, was that the former involved the successful establishment of a home, rather than simply a move to new accommodation. Indeed for some people it would be appropriate to encourage them to establish a home within a hostel if it were of a suitable standard. In arguing this Dant and Deacon were supporting Green's advocacy of what he described as a 'deliberately naive' understanding of what resettlement work is: 'helping people to decide where to live and then helping them to live there' (Green, 1985, p.97). As Resettlement Officer for Camden, Green was responsible for the rehousing of the residents of the large Arlington House hostel. The strategy adopted laid great emphasis upon the provision of advice and information in addition to the assessment of residents:

> The reason why I lay so much stress on generating conditions for free choice and why the information exercises are important is that people are sometimes driven by rather questionable motives to apply for rehousing. If we can reassure them that they do not have to move, if we can topple the flat off its false position at the top of the housing hierarchy, if we can confirm people's suspicions that, yes, financially they might be worse off if they go and live in a flat – if we do all these things and someone decides to stay in the hostel but with greater clarity of purpose and a stronger sense of security, then I think that valuable resettlement work has been performed. (p.97)

A further corollary of the distinction between rehousing and resettlement is that a person who moved on again after being rehoused had not necessarily failed to resettle. He or she could be abandoning his or her home, but they could equally be moving home to another property.

The central point to emerge from the Leeds study, however, was 'success' or 'failure' in these terms depended little upon the acquisition of domestic skills:

> helping people to settle is less about whether they can manage in the home, as about whether they feel they are in the right place, whether they can identify with the place as a home, and whether they can maintain a lifestyle congruent with having a settled home. (Dant and Deacon, 1989, p.71)

In some cases the changes that would be required to maintain such a lifestyle would be considerably more demanding than learning how to cook. In broad terms, establishing a home was

> a process of integration or re-integration into the cultural system that they have existed on the margins of. The strategies that they have used for survival in the marginal context (petty crime, excessive alcohol use, moving on) have to be abandoned or adapted. (p.106)

This transition could not be effected without support and in the absence of a range of housing options. But nor would it be possible unless the individuals concerned were willing to meet the demands made upon them. Single homelessness was not a simple matter of individual pathology, but nor was it solely a housing problem. The staff of the Leeds Shaftesbury Project had been forced to address questions of personal behaviour – as had those working for the CRS projects (Tilt and Denford, 1986, p.35).

The diverse needs of single homeless people

Dant and Deacon's argument was that the 'good housekeeping' model constituted a limited view of the support needs of people who were being resettled, and that this in turn reflected a partial explanation of the causes of homelessness. More recently, Nicholas Pleace has reviewed the findings of a range of studies in Britain and the United States and put forward a valuable typology of the needs of single homeless people. He divides these into five categories (Pleace, 1995, pp.6–8):

- E housing needs
    - E support needs
    - E health needs
- E personal support needs
- E daily living skills
- E financial needs
- E social needs.

The relative importance of such needs will vary enormously between different subgroups of homeless single people. As Pleace argues, some will require little more than access to suitable and affordable housing, while for others the provision of accommodation without support may well exacerbate their problems.

> In short, existing research indicates that single homelessness is varied and complex in nature and must sometimes be addressed as a community care problem, sometimes as a problem of individual alienation, sometimes as being related to a lack of daily living skills and always, at least in part, as a housing problem. (Pleace, 1995, p.8)

The importance of formulating policies which recognise and respond to the diverse needs of single homeless people is illustrated by the closure of the former DSS resettlement units.

The closure of the resettlement units: a case study in resettlement
The closure programme

In 1985 the then Department of Health and Social Security was still responsible for administration of 23 resettlement units, 8 of which were in London. These units were direct-access hostels whose official purpose was to provide 'persons without a settled way of life', with 'temporary board and lodging with a view to influencing them to lead a more settled life' (Deacon and Jones, 1988, p.169).

The resettlement units had few supporters outside the civil service unions whose members were employed in them. They were seen by groups such as CHAR and by academic commentators as exemplifying all the defects of large hostels and as having failed almost completely to encourage their residents to settle down. Moreover, their administration by the DHSS was an anachronism at a time when homelessness was recognised to be a problem of housing and – worse still – the continued role of the DHSS constituted a vestigial link with the casual wards of the nineteenth-century poor law. The DHSS itself believed the units to be overstaffed and inefficient, and saw their closure as a swift and painless way of reducing the size of the public sector.

It is not surprising, therefore, that the DHSS announced in February 1985 that it intended to move towards the closure of the resettlement units, nor that this announcement provoked little protest. The initial strategy of the DHSS was straightforward. It would redirect the monies spent on the units to voluntary agencies already working with single homeless people, and thereby enable them to expand their existing activities. Voluntary organisations, it was argued, 'were better equipped to provide the kind of informal, non-restrictive accommodation and atmosphere most likely to encourage their users to learn how to achieve a greater measure of independence'. The closure of the units, then, would not lead to the direct resettlement of their users, but to their transfer to an alternative, more effective mechanism for resettlement.

To achieve this, each DHSS regional office was to establish a review team, comprising representatives of statutory and voluntary bodies along with others with relevant expertise. The review teams were to assess the needs in their areas, consider bids from voluntary agencies and make recommendations. In essence, they were to ensure fair play as the voluntary bodies competed for the funds available. It was not envisaged that the discussions would be either prolonged or contentious, and the eight 'most dilapidated' units were to be shut by March 1988, and the remainder shortly after.

In the event, however, the closure programme turned out to be an extraordinary political saga which at various times included a virtual stand-off between the government and the review teams over the funding of the replacement provision, continual confusion as to whether that provision should be seen as a direct replacement for the units or a general response to the needs of single homeless people in the area concerned, and sharp shifts in government policy from one which gave absolute priority to the outright closure of the units to one which encouraged their transfer to the voluntary sector, and back again, and back again. In early 1989 the closure programme appeared about to collapse but the establishment of the Resettlement Agency in May of that year brought a greater clarity of purpose and a welcome sense of urgency. The Agency adopted a twin-track approach towards replacement provision; implementing the proposals which appeared to offer the largest number of beds in the shortest time scale and effectively ignoring the review teams which were proving awkward. The final policy, however, did not emerge until February 1992 when Ann Widdecombe, Parliamentary Under-secretary, announced that the units which had not yet closed would be transferred directly to organisations with skills and experience in caring for single homeless people. Transfer would be in response to a tendering process with the Agency continuing to provide funding to organisations taking over the resettlement units. In the event, 11 units were transferred including that in Sheffield which was taken over by St Anne's in April 1995. The remainder all have been closed, with the units in Leeds and Glasgow being the last two to shut in April 1996 (Social Security Committee, 1994–95, p.13).

The story of the closure programme has been told in more detail elsewhere (Vincent, Deacon and Walker, 1995). The focus here is upon the lessons of that programme for resettlement work in general, and the remainder of the chapter draws upon a study of the consequences of the closure of the unit in Alvaston, near Derby.

Alvaston Resettlement Unit

Alvaston was one of the last units to be shut before the policy changed to one of transferring their management to the voluntary sector. The standard of accommodation was poor: World War II nissan huts with dormitory spurs off a spine corridor. There had once been over 100 residents but Alvaston had a nominal capacity of 74 bedspaces immediately before closure. One spur had been turned into flatlets for resettlement work and there was a workshop and a small farm which in its heyday supplied the kitchen with vegetables.

Unlike most resettlement units, Alvaston had succeeded in offering a mixture of resettlement models on one site. The flat scheme provided scope for residents to acquire domestic skills that may have been lacking, and support was provided once residents found accommodation in the wider community, although this was made possible largely through the commitment and enthusiasm of staff. More importantly perhaps, the Alvaston regime also afforded sanctuary for large numbers of people. The door was rarely closed on anyone, residents were given a second, third and fourth chance and, for some, Alvaston was home.

Who stayed at Alvaston?

An analysis of the unit records on all the 514 men who had used Alvaston in the 12 months before closure proved to be a rich source of data. In general, the information gleaned from the records regarding the characteristics and experiences of individual residents confirmed the findings of other studies. This was true, for example, of the importance of family breakdown as a factor precipitating homelessness, the poor state of health of many residents, and the considerable amount of time that they had spent in children's homes and other institutions.

A more striking point to emerge, however, was the sheer diversity of the people who used Alvaston. Over a third of them had been on the road for at least ten years, and nearly a fifth had led an unsettled life for more than twenty years. On the other hand, at least one-third had been on the road for less than a year, and 5 per cent had become homeless on the day they entered Alvaston.

By far the most striking findings to emerge from the analysis of the records held at Alvaston, however, related to the number and length of stays. All told, some 804 stays were recorded in the admissions book between 1 April 1991 and the final closure. A little over a third of these stays lasted for a single night and half for three nights or less. It is clear, then, that the majority of the men who used Alvaston in this period had stayed for only a very short time. This does not mean, however, that the majority of the men who were resident on any one day had only just arrived. On the contrary, an analysis of those staying on the night of 1 October 1991 showed that 70 per cent of them had been in Alvaston for over a month and only 2 per cent for less than one week.

The reason for this discrepancy is that men who stayed for long periods gradually took over a large proportion of the bed places, whereas men using Alvaston for short periods followed each other into the same beds. In other words the 'stock' of men resident on any one night was not representative of the 'flow' of men through the unit over a year. This is critical in understanding the use which was made of the unit and the functions which it performed. For example, a quarter of the men who visited Alvaston in 1991/2 stayed for one night, but they accounted for less than 1 per cent of the bed spaces that were occupied during the year. In contrast, the 6 per cent of men who stayed for more than six months occupied 43 per cent of the bed spaces which were utilised. Even the 11 per cent who made repeated short visits to Alvaston – men who might traditionally, if erroneously, be considered to be the archetypal users of resettlement units – accounted for only 6 per cent of the bed spaces used.

What is of particular significance for policy is the fact that a unit like Alvaston, which appears from the outside to have a very stable population, should still be meeting the immediate and short-term needs of so many men, and that many of these short-term users had become homeless relatively recently.

The replacement programme
It is necessary to appreciate the diverse uses that were made of Alvaston in order to understand the impact of its closure. In formal terms only those who were resident in the unit on the night of 10 December 1991 were eligible for rehousing in the accommodation which comprised the replacement package. In practice, however, 20 men were placed in alternative accommodation before that date, and 10 men who arrived after 10 December 1991 were also

rehoused. The crucial point, however, is that the great majority of the 64 who were actively placed as part of the closure programme were long-term residents – 82 per cent had lived in Alvaston for more than a month and 33 per cent for over six months. This, of course, followed directly from the use of one particular night to determine eligibility. While it is to be expected that long-term residents would need to be found accommodation, this strategy nevertheless meant that the replacement provision served only a minority of the Alvaston constituency. Only five short-stay residents were actively placed, even though this group constituted 46 per cent of users.

The eventual closure of Alvaston took place over a three-month period from 10 December 1991. The package of replacement accommodation which had been finally agreed with the review team comprised four different schemes offering a range of resettlement regimes. In Tilt and Denford's terms, Somerville House operated an 'assertive and interventionistic' policy while the others provided different forms of 'sanctuary'. They all, however, imposed a much stricter regime upon their residents than had Alvaston, especially the dry house which evicted anyone who resumed drinking. Hartington House in Derby was the nearest to a direct replacement for Alvaston, although here too house rules were strictly enforced.

The consequences of the closure

Evidence of the effects of the closure was collected in a series of interviews with residents before and after the event, and by means of a tracing exercise which sought to gather information on all the 62 men who had been actively placed and a further 15 who had been interviewed at an early stage of the study. In all something was learned of the whereabouts of 72 of these men and 15 of them were interviewed again.

The broad outcome is indicated by Table 5.1 which records the outcomes for just the 62 men who were actively placed. (The total number of moves recorded is 64. Two men appeared twice because they were twice found accommodation during the period). Eighteen were still in the accommodation to which they moved and 44 had moved on again. Strikingly, *none* of the men who moved to the designated replacement accommodation remained there after a year. In contrast, 7 of the 10 men who moved into local authority accommodation had stayed put and so had 7 of the 12 men who were rehoused in the private sector.

There are, however, two very important qualifications. First, someone who has 'stayed put' has not necessarily been resettled in any meaningful sense. One of the men who had stayed in Sheffield Resettlement Unit, for example, was living exactly as he had before except that instead of paying periodic visits to Alvaston he spent short periods sleeping rough in a neighbouring village. Conversely, a man who has moved on again may have done so to establish a home elsewhere. One, for example, spent a short time in a hostel in Derby and then moved to a shared house where he lived for nearly a year. Whilst there he began a relationship with a woman and eventually went to live with her.

The second qualification is that the agencies represented in Table 5.1 have different objectives. Some seek to offer sanctuary, but others do not perceive

Table 5.1 Resettlement: destinations and outcomes

	Number of men resettled	Number who stayed	Number who moved on
Replacement Accommodation			
Somerville House, Nottingham	7	0	7
Second Base, Nottingham	2	0	2
London Road Dry House, Derby	3	0	3
Hartington House, Derby	18	0	18
Resettlment Units			
Leicester	1	0	1
Sheffield	2	2	0
Voluntary Sector			
Hostel, Stoke-on-Trent	1	*	*
Dry House, Derby	1	0	1
Carr Gomm House, Derby	2	2	0
Dry House, Birmingham	1	0	1
Hostel, Nottingham	1	0	1
Housing Association			
Hostel and Move-On, Derby	1	0	1
Flat, Derby	2	0	2
Derby City Council			
Flat, Derby	9	6	3
Sheltered bedsit, Derby	1	1	0
Private Sector			
Residential home, Skegness	3	0	3
Residential homes (3), Derby	5	3	2
Residential home, Scotland	1	1	0
Own house, Derby	1	1	0
Caring landlady, Derby	2	2	0
Total	64	18	45

* not traced

themselves as providing long-term accommodation and would not expect their residents to stay for as long as a year.

All told, perhaps 16 of the 62 men were in more stable housing circumstances – and therefore closer towards a 'return to a more normal lifestyle' – than they had been when at Alvaston. Which factors – if any – exerted a major influence upon the pattern of outcomes? The stricter regimes encountered in the replacement accommodation played their part. All three residents who went to the dry house began drinking again and were either asked to leave or left of their own accord. Nine of the eighteen going to Hartington House, for example, were evicted, mostly within a month because of heavy drinking or breaking other house rules.

Age and prior length of stay at Alvaston also appear to be important indicators of 'success'. Seven of the nine men who moved into local authority flats, for example, had been in the unit for more than six months, as had all of the men who went to Carr Gomm House and six of the nine who moved to residential care homes. Similarly, all of the men in residential care homes were elderly, as were two of those in Carr Gomm House and those with a caring landlady.

More fundamentally, however, the experiences of those who had formerly lived in Alvaston confirmed that the key to successful resettlement was the establishment of a lifestyle congruent with having a settled home. It was a matter of occupation rather than boredom, of companionship rather than loneliness, of a sense of belonging rather than of isolation. The interviews with those who had left Alvaston provided vivid examples of both these extremes.

Some of the men who had stayed put had succeeded in maintaining those aspects of life in the unit which they most valued. Three of the men in local authority flats went fishing together regularly, and others had acquired pets and developed new hobbies and interests. Two of the men in Carr Gomm House, for example, had obtained qualifications in gardening and were also undertaking voluntary work. In the case of other men, however, the return to the road had been rapid, with most citing boredom, loneliness and drink as the precipitating factors.

The lessons of Alvaston
Any discussion of the implications of the closure of Alvaston for resettlement in general must begin by acknowledging that those who made regular use of the former resettlement units constituted a discreet subset of the single

homeless population, and one which previous studies had found to be particularly hard to resettle. That said, it is still surely remarkable that a year after the unit closed not one of the former residents was living in the accommodation which was supposed to have replaced it. The principal reason for this was the fact that the replacement provision all but excluded the former residents either through formal admittance criteria or the imposition of house rules that they were unable to conform to.

Conversely, the Alvaston regime had allowed some men to stay for considerable periods. Most had been travellers or otherwise homeless for decades and they tended to appreciate both the company and the scope for purposive activity that Alvaston offered. The workshop and farm at Alvaston may seem to some commentators to be a unwelcome link with the poor law, but to many of those interviewed they provided an opportunity for a meaningful and structured use of time which was much missed in the replacement accommodation. Another group of men who said they regretted the closure of the unit were those who had made frequent short visits. It is, of course, very important to view such findings in context and not to give the impression that either Alvaston or resettlement units in general were viewed more favourably than they in fact were. It should be remembered that some respondents were only too glad to leave Alvaston, and that conditions in many of the other units were markedly less congenial than they were in Alvaston. It is also possible that the disruption and stress generated by the closure process lead some former residents to take a somewhat rosy view of the their days in the unit. Even when all these qualifications have been made, however, it is still clear that some respondents missed acutely the regime at Alvaston.

Similar points have been made by Paul Winstanley, Chief Executive of the Resettlement Agency, in a particularly thoughtful memorandum to the Commons Social Security Committee. Mr Winstanley began by noting that although conditions in the former unit in Camberwell were truly appalling it was always full. In contrast the experience of the Resettlement Agency in London in recent years was that 'we have consistently had empty bedspaces' even though people were sleeping on the street. This raises the question as to why some of the 'traditional client group' of the Units were now 'often choosing to sleep rough despite the availability of hostel accommodation'. The answer, Mr Winstanley suggested, lay in the 'conflict between the characteristics of this group and the aims of the hostels which would seem appropriate for them'. Such conflicts could be generated, for example, between 'clients with low self esteem and a desire for anonymity' and service provision 'that includes high standard accommodation and an expectation that the client will adapt to co-existing as part of a small group within the hostel'. Further problems arose from the notion of resettlement as 'a commitment to a changed lifestyle'. Indeed for those unable to recall anything other than an unsettled lifestyle 'the idea of resettlement must be confusing and even intimidating' (Social Security Committee, 1994–95, p.24).

Conclusion: the implications for policy

The obvious conclusion to be drawn from the material discussed in this chapter is that the diversity of the needs of single homeless people should be matched by a range of provision. This is a policy which is much easier to state than to implement. It requires that a range of options be made available, encompassing group homes and various forms of 'special needs' provision as well as independent houses and flats. Crucially, however, it also requires that direct-access hostels continue to play an important role, although the design and management of such hostels remains a much neglected issue (Willcocks, Peace and Kellaher, 1987).

The significance of direct-access accommodation arises in part from the need to provide a first port of call for the newly homeless – but also to cater for those who have decided to continue to travel. Again it is important that this latter point is not misunderstood. To suggest that some of the former residents of Alvaston returned to travel by choice is not to reinforce the stereotype of resettlement unit users as feckless itinerants who either have no wish to settle down or are incapable of doing so. Far from it. The Alvaston study documented many examples of successful resettlement. At the same time it has to be recognised that some respondents described themselves as travelling men and spoke very clearly about their wish to continue to travel, at least for the time being. It is not simply a question of a 'forced unsettledness' as was claimed in the report quoted earlier. Moreover, if travelling is not viewed as a problem to be 'cured' by resettlement then more positive attention can be given to the needs of those with recognised difficulties of alcohol abuse and mental ill health.

This, of course, relates to the broader point made at the beginning of the chapter about the need to strike an appropriate balance between individual and structural factors in explaining the persistence of homelessness. As Christopher Jencks has again argued, the homeless are not just passive victims. They make choices like everyone else. The choices open to the homeless are far worse than those open to most Americans, but they are still choices. (Jencks, 1994, p.104)

This applies equally to Britain. The essence of resettlement, then, is to improve the choices open to homeless people. The focus should be upon the enhancement of chosen lifestyles. For some this will mean providing access to independent living in houses or flats together with help with 'housekeeping skills'. For others, however, that would create too great a risk of isolation and poverty, and for some of those who formerly used the resettlement units it will mean hostels which provide adequate facilities, a measure of anonymity, opportunities for occupation, and sensitive management.

References

Anderson, I. (1994) *Access to Housing for Low Income Single People.* York: Centre for Housing Policy, University of York.

Anderson, I., Kemp, P. and Quilgars, D. (1993) *Single Homeless People.* London: HMSO.

CHAR (1983) *Single and Homeless the Facts.* London: CHAR.

Crossley, B. and Denmark, J.C. (1969) 'Community care – a study of the psychiatric morbidity of a Salvation Army hostel.' *British Journal of Sociology 4*, 20, 446–449.

Crowther, M.A. (1981) *The Workhouse System.* London: Methuen.

Dant, T. and Deacon, A. (1989) *From Hostels to Homes: The Rehousing of Single Homeless People.* Aldershot: Avebury.

Deacon, A. and Jones, H. (1988) 'Policies for the single homeless: the case of the DHSS Resettlement Units.' In M. Brenton and C. Ungerson (eds) *The Yearbook of Social Policy in Britain 1987.* Harlow: Longman.

Donnison, D.V. (1991) *A Radical Agenda.* London: Rivers Oram Press.

Drake, M. (1985) 'The housing of homeless single people.' *Housing Review 3*, 34 96.

Drake, M., O'Brien, M. and Biebuyck, T. (1982) *Single and Homeless.* London: HMSO.

Duncan, S. and Downey, P. (1985) *Settling Down.* London: HMSO.

Garside, D., Grimshaw, R. And Ward, F. (1990) *No Place Like Home.* London: Department of the Environment.

GLC (1985) *The JART Experience 1980–1985.* London: GLC.

Green, J. (1985) 'The resettlement process from Arlington House.' *Housing Review 3*, 34, 97–98.

Holmes, C. (1986) 'The worsening crisis of single homelessness.' In P. Malpass (ed) *The Housing Crisis.* London: Croom Helm.

Jencks, C. (1994) *The Homeless.* Cambridge, MA: Harvard University Press.

Krafchik, M. (1983) 'Unemployment and vagrancy in the 1930s.' *Journal of Social Policy 12*, 2 195–214.

Lewisham Single Housing Group (1981) *Carrington House: Under Radical Review.* London: CHAR.

National Assistance Board. (1966) *Report of the National Assistance Board for 1965.* Cmnd 3046. London: HMSO.

Pleace, N. (1995) *Housing Vulnerable Single Homeless People.* York: Centre for Housing Policy, University of York.

Social Security Committee (1994–95) *Fifth Report: The Work of the Department of Social Security and its Agencies,* House of Commons Session 1994–95. London: HMSO.

Tilt, A. and Denford, S. (1986) *The Camberwell Scheme: Experiences of the First Three Years.* London: DHSS.

Vincent, J., Deacon, A. and Walker, R. (1995) *Homeless Single Men: Roads to Resettlement?* Aldershot: Avebury.

Watson, S. and Austerberry, H. (1986) *Housing and Homelessness: A Feminist Perspective.* London: Routledge and Kegan Paul.

Willcocks, D., Peace, S. and Kellaher, L. (1987) *Private Lives in Public Places.* London: Tavistock.

Further reading

Duffy, J. (1985) *Re-Housing Hostel Residents. The Experience in Glasgow.* Glasgow: Glasgow Council for the Single Homeless.

Duncan, S., Downey, P. and Finch, H. (1983) *A Home of Their Own.* London: Department of Environment.

Garside, D., Grimshaw, R. and Ward, F. (1990) *No Place like Home.* London: Department of Environment.

National Audit Office (1992) *Department of Social Security: Resettlement Agency.* London: NAO.

CHAPTER 6

Racism, Ethnicity and Youth Homelessness

Ian Law, Jacqui Davies, Stephen Lyle and Alan Deacon

Introduction

The purpose of this chapter is to examine the nature and extent of youth homelessness, particularly amongst black and minority ethnic communities. In so doing it is important to acknowledge the ways in which the housing market constrains and influences young black people's experiences. The character and extent of racial discrimination in the various sectors of the housing market constitute one of the most well-established aspects of racial inequality in modern Britain (Law, 1996). Discrimination in the supply of housing has taken a variety of forms. Blatant exclusion, the 'steering' of housing choices of minority households and discrimination in the provision of information about housing opportunities by estate agents, accommodation agencies and housing managers has been well documented. The operation of indirect discrimination in the regulation of access to council housing, housing association properties and mortgages has also been well documented (Braham, Rattansi and Skellington, 1992; Commission for Racial Equality, 1983, 1984a, 1984b, 1985, 1988a, 1988b, 1989a, 1989b, 1989c, 1989d, 1990a, 1990b, 1990c, 1991, 1992, 1993a, 1993b, 1993c). The significance of such discrimination in accounting for and explaining the reproduction of racial and ethnic inequalities in housing opportunities and outcomes has, however, frequently been overstated, with a tendency for such arguments to slip into monocausal accounts which emphasise the structural determination of such practices in limiting provision, or supply, in the housing market. Here, the operation of racism, elaborated in its subjective, institutional and structural forms, provides an 'easy' explanation for the development and persistence of racial inequality (Ginsburg, 1992). The development of a more complex and holistic account of racial inequalities in the housing market must also address a range of other factors, as studies by Sarre, Phillips and Skellington (1989), Smith and Hill (1991) and Harrison (1995) illustrate. The complexity of patterns of demand needs to be taken into account with consideration of preferences, aspirations, choices and household strategies. Here, real differences within and between ethnic groups in locational choices, tenure preferences, patterns of household formation and patterns of homelessness need to be given greater weight and attention. Second, general questions of prevailing market conditions, patterns of housing finance, investment and legislative and policy interventions must be analysed and their differential impact on racialised groups needs to be assessed. Third, linkages between housing and other structures of racial and ethnic inequality need to be made, particularly the labour market, education, health, wealth and political power.

The growth in the level of homelessness in the last two decades reflects the widening of general social inequalities and therefore we would expect to find significant ethnic differentials reflecting those found in wider patterns of income, wealth and housing inequality. Over a third of those classified as non-white, in the 1990 General Household Survey, are in households with gross incomes (adjusted for family size) in the poorest fifth, compared with 18 per cent of whites (Hills, 1995). The higher probability of low incomes amongst non-whites is particularly striking given the relatively small numbers of pensioners in this group (as they tend to have low incomes generally). Bangladeshi, Pakistani and West Indian households, in declining order of probability, are particularly likely to be on low incomes. Analysis of 1991 Census data show that over half of Bangladeshis were living in wards which were in the most deprived tenth nationally ranked by unemployment, economic inactivity or lack of car ownership (Green, 1994). Levels of car ownership can also be used to indicate income and Census data show that Indian and Chinese households had higher rates of ownership than whites (76.8% and 70.6% compared with 67%) with very low rates amongst blacks (44.9%) and Bangladeshis (39.1%). The widening in income inequalities over the last two decades is evident across minority ethnic groups, with Indian and Chinese households diverging in their socio-economic trajectories from the position of Bangladeshis, Pakistanis and black (as Census defined) people. In addition, the widening of income inequalities within each of these groups is likely to be occurring and at differing rates. (Evidence on ethnicity by income is poor, the Family Expenditure Survey does not collect ethnicity data, the General Household Survey collects ethnicity data but minority ethnic samples are too small for reliable analysis of individual groups and the DSS Family Resources Survey which will provide some useful data is not yet available.) As regards marketable wealth, this correlates positively with income and age and given the concentration of minorities in the lower end of the income distribution and in the younger end of the age structure we can propose a similar complex pattern of wealth inequalities across ethnic groups to that of income with the condition that generally wealth inequalities are much greater (Joseph Rowntree Foundation, 1995). Given the preceding discussion, we would therefore anticipate that Bangladeshi, Pakistani and black people would be particularly hardest hit by the growth of homelessness, with lower levels amongst white, Indian and Chinese people. The significantly younger age structure of minority ethnic groups and withdrawal of benefits for young people, particularly 16- to 18-year-olds would also indicate the potential for the growth of homelessness amongst young, single people from the most vulnerable minority groups.

Over twenty years ago the Community Relations Commission highlighted the problems of homelessness, particularly amongst young blacks in Lambeth and Birmingham, and established the key linkage with unemployment (CRC, 1974). More recent research (Coles and Craine, 1995; TUC, 1995, 1996; Amin, 1996; Hagell and Shaw, 1996; Wilkinson and Mulgan, 1996) has confirmed the worsening of this linkage and has shown that young African-Caribbean and Asian people are experiencing longer and more 'fractured' transitions from school to employment, in establishing families and in securing their own accommodation. This overall picture conceals substantial variations and the importance of recognising first the diverging socio-economic trajectories of groups within the black and Asian categories, and second the diverging socio-economic trajectories of groups of people within each minority ethnic group, as seen in Labour Force Survey data on education, employment and housing outcomes (Law, 1996), is now being recognised. In contrast to the deconstruction of ethnic categories in social analysis, it is important to acknowledge the common impact of racism on many children's lives in contributing to a stressful transition from childhood to adulthood, as a recent ChildLine (1996) study has shown. This study emphasised the shame and despair experienced by children suffering blatant, unrelenting, openly racist harassment and bullying, particularly at school but also within families.

Research evidence on ethnic differences in youth homelessness

This chapter draws substantially upon findings from a recent joint research project between the Federation of Black Housing Organisations, CHAR (Campaign for the Single Homeless) and the 'Race' and Public Policy Research Unit at the University of Leeds which investigated the perceptions and experiences of homelessness across white, black and Asian groups outside London (Davies and Lyle *et al.*, 1996). As well as focusing on young black and minority ethnic people, this study has concentrated on provincial England rather than the capital city. This is in response to the finding in a previous national survey of homeless people that there are now more homeless young people outside of London than within (Randall, 1994). The research began in September 1994 and was completed in November 1995. This research strengthens the findings of previous studies; black minority ethnic groups are found to be over-represented amongst the residents of hostels and bed and breakfast hotels, and particularly amongst young people and women in such accommodation, they are also much more likely to have previously stayed with friends rather than to have been sleeping rough (Elam, 1992; Anderson, Kemp and Quilgars, 1993; Randall and Brown, 1993; Strathdee, 1993). There are three particularly useful sources of information on the ethnicity of young homeless people. The first and most important is the recent report *Single Homeless People* produced by the Centre for Housing Policy at the University of York. This presents the findings of a representative survey of users of accommodation and services for single homeless people in five London boroughs and five local authority areas outside London (Anderson *et al.*, 1993). The second source is the evaluation of the Rough Sleepers Initiative (RSI) in London, which was undertaken by Randall and Brown (1993). The third source consists of a range of studies of particular localities – primarily in London – and specific forms of accommodation (Scott, 1991; Elam, 1992; Smith and Gilford, 1993; Strathdee, 1993).

The results of these studies are strikingly consistent. It is clear that people from black ethnic minority groups are over-represented amongst the residents of hostels and bed and breakfast hotels (B&B), and particularly so amongst young people and women in such accommodation. *Single Homeless*

People reports, for example, that 26 per cent of all residents were from ethnic minority groups, but that this proportion rose to 44 per cent of 16/17-year-olds and 38 per cent of all those under 25 (Anderson *et al.*, 1993, p.106). Almost a half of all women in hostels and B&B were from black or other ethnic minority groups (p.101). Conversely, nearly a half of all the people from ethnic minority groups were under 25, and over a third of them were women (p.111). These findings confirm those of the RSI study, of research on homelessness in London conducted at the University of Surrey in 1988–89, and of Ye-Myint's detailed study in Tower Hamlets (Moore *et al.*, 1991; Ye-Myint, 1992). Both the York and RSI surveys found that hostel and B&B residents from ethnic minority groups were more likely to have stayed previously with friends and were much less likely to have slept rough. This may be from fears of racist attacks, but it may also reflect the different characteristics of white and ethnic minority residents since both young people and women were less likely to sleep rough regardless of ethnic origin. The over-representation of young people from ethnic minority groups revealed by these studies is due in part to the fact they have been conducted in areas where such communities form a relatively large proportion of the population, and a further factor in Central London is the high number of refugees or asylum seekers in hostels and B&Bs (Campbell and Devore, 1990; Anderson *et al.*, 1993). Nevertheless, there is evidence that young black people are similarly over-represented amongst the homeless in other English cities and towns. A recent study by the London-based homeless agency Centrepoint found that 44 per cent of the 729 young people admitted to their hostels in 1993 defined themselves as black or mixed race. Fifty-one per cent of black hostel dwellers included in the survey were female. The same study also revealed that young black people were less likely to have ever slept rough than their white counterparts (20% of young black people, 47% of young white people) and were also less likely to have ever used a squat (4% of young black people, 22% of young white people). Young black people were however, more likely to have stayed with friends before arriving at Centrepoint (37% of young black people, 20% of young white people).

Review of national data sets by Davies *et al.*, (1996) – which included Shelter's housing aid centre data, CHAR's survey of hostels and local government P1E returns, and dialogue with relevant agencies – has confirmed this pattern outside London, and particularly highlighted disproportionate levels of homelessness amongst young black minority ethnic groups in the East Midlands, the West Midlands and West Yorkshire. Smith and Gilford (1993) collected information on 2738 young people in housing need in Birmingham. A quarter were 'roofless' (living in hostels, offered hostel places or sleeping rough), another four out of ten were homeless or potentially homeless and the remaining third were urgently seeking accommodation or housing advice. Nearly a third (32%) were from minority ethnic groups and this is higher than might be expected. The study identified young people of African-Caribbean origin to be at particular risk of homelessness as they were nearly 12 per cent of the survey population but only 5 per cent of Birmingham's 16–24 population. This latter estimate is based on census information and is likely to significantly underenumerate the number of young men generally due particularly to low rates of form completion and the impact of the poll tax. Taking this into account, the risk difference is likely to be lower than that suggested. Whereas Asian young people were 20 per cent of the 16–24 Census population and only 8 per cent of this study's sample, this may indicate the greater extent of 'hidden' homelessness amongst these groups which requires further investigation.

Young discounted voices

In seeking to examine ethnic differences amongst those experiencing youth homelessness, group discussions were held at two hostels in West Yorkshire and one in the East Midlands, and 126 young people were individually interviewed. Individual respondents were contacted through agencies working with the relevant group – typically housing associations and advice centres – and through outreach work using community contacts in three areas: West Midlands, West Yorkshire and the East Midlands. This sample included 53 African-Caribbeans, 46 whites, 46 Pakistanis, 8 Indians and 5 Bangaldeshis. Young Asians were the most difficult to contact, reflecting a variety of factors including a reluctance on the part of Asian communities to recognise the significance of youth homelessness and an insistence that such problems were dealt with by and within the community. The preference of young homeless Asians for 'move-on' locations away from known communities where they felt they could be relatively anonymous reflects these tensions. Such tensions and preferences were particularly evident in cases of domestic violence.

Becoming homeless

It was found that causes of homelessness were very similar for both white, African-Caribbean and Asian young people and that the most common reason for homelessness was a crisis in family relationships which led to the household splitting (accounting for 44% of men and 21% of women in this sample). As a result family relationships often subsequently improved. Many young people said that they were keen to assert their independence which often brought them into conflict with parents who had very different ideas about how their sons and daughters should be conducting their lives. It was often difficult to distinguish between those young people who were 'kicked out' and those who could not continue to live at home and left of their own accord. It was clear however that the situation was intolerable for both parties and the strain eventually led to breakdown.

> I lived with my mum and she wouldn't let me do what I wanted to with my friends and such like. So our relationship broke down. I then went to live with my dad and that didn't work out, so I went to stay with friends. Then I went back home to my mum and one night she asked me to leave and I knew that was it – so I left. (Female resident, Hostel 1)

> I was at my mum's and she couldn't cope with me. I was too much trouble for her. She did not like me drinking and one day she asked me to leave. (Male resident, Hostel 3)

> From when I was 15 my mum used to give me orders like telling me what time to come in on a night. Then one day she said you think you're a big person now, then it's time for you to go. I said OK and left. I went from friend to friend for about four months and then one friend put me up until I was 16, then I came here. (Male resident, Hostel 1)

Many young people stated that they regretted the 'bust-up' had happened and many regretted that they were not given time to prepare themselves and plan what their course of action was going to be.

> I would have preferred to have had time to prepare to leave home so that it could have been done properly – I prefer to set myself up first, but sometimes there's no choice, you can't do that and you've just got to leave. (Male resident, Hostel 1)

Despite their regret at their relationship with parents breaking down and their subsequent homelessness, many of the young people felt that they had made the right decision leaving home when they did. For many their relationship with their parent(s) improved considerably as a result of their leaving. They said that to have stayed would have created more serious tensions that may have become irreparable.

> My relationship with my mum is better because my mum had to let go, she couldn't control my life anymore so once she accepted that, things got better. I respect and appreciate her a lot more now. (Female resident, Hostel 1)

> I left and had to find somewhere like this to live – and now we get on. (Male resident, Hostel 1)

One in five respondents became homeless as a result of threats of violence or actual physical violence and/or sexual violence, including instances of harassment in the neighbourhood. This was particularly significant for Indian and Pakistani women where the proportion was one in three. A small but noteworthy group of young men also reported physical/sexual abuse as a cause of becoming homeless.

A third of African-Caribbeans and whites had been in a children's home at some point in their lives, compared with a sixth of Asians, with twice the proportion of men experiencing such care and overall 14 per cent of respondents saying they had never had a place they felt to be home. Reports from those leaving institutional care show the abrupt shift from one form of accommodation to another.

> I was never at home actually. I was forced out. I was 16 years of age, in care which was a little hostel place like here. They taught you how to cook and things like that. It didn't work out though. One day they [social services] packed up some of my things, put me in a car and dropped me off at a hostel. (Male resident, Hostel 1)

> I last lived in Harlesden [North-West London] in 1991 but I've just done a long sentence from when I was 14 and they sent me to a secure unit. When I was getting out, I told my social worker that I wanted to come up here [Leeds] and they told me about this place. I came up, saw it was clean and said yes. (Male resident, Hostel 3)

First stop for help

Demand for agency support, from either statutory or voluntary agencies was higher amongst white youth and lowest amongst Asian youth who felt greater confidence with and reliance upon informal community networks. In general, half of those interviewed did not know where to go for advice when they first became homeless. Many young people relied upon informal networks, 'word-of-mouth' or knowing another person who had been homeless and who could explain how the 'system' works.

> I was staying with friends in Liverpool for a few months. I didn't know where to go for advice in Liverpool, I had nowhere to run. There might be hostels for black people in Liverpool, but I certainly did not know where to find them. (Female resident, Hostel 2)

> I found out because I knew someone who used to live here. I used to visit them and then when I came here, they gave me a place the same week. (Male resident, Hostel 1)

Despite young black homeless people stating their reluctance to approach housing advice centres, many black-run hostels' monitoring statistics show that referrals from such centres are in fact increasing.

Staying with friends/relatives

This was a more common strategy amongst African-Caribbean and Asian youth. About half of blacks, compared with a quarter of whites, cited this as their previous accommodation before entering a hostel, which together with sleeping rough was seen as a last resort.

> I was staying with friends in lots of different flats, even one in Barnsley, before coming here. (Male resident, Hostel 1)

> I went to stay with friends, certain friends who I knew would help. It was a matter of self-pride and they've given me the chance to get out. (Female resident, Hostel 2)

Also blacks were more likely to stay with their friends or relatives for longer periods than young white homeless people.

> I was homeless for three months in —————, but before that I was staying with friends in Liverpool for a few months. (Female resident, Hostel 2)

> ...I was about 15 [when I left home] and I went from friend to friend for about four months and then one friend put me up until I was 16. (Male resident, Hostel 1)

> I've lived in about three or four different places and I've never signed-on [the dole] ... I didn't really want to take that money, its a matter of self-pride ... I think in total I've lived in 20 places before I came here. (Male resident, Hostel 1)

Rough sleeping

Sleeping rough in doorways, overturned sofas, cars, stations or other places was common amongst men and relatively rare amongst African-Caribbean and Asian women. Of those interviewed, nearly all white men had slept rough, in comparison with half of all black men and one-fifth of all black women. Gender differences were greatest amongst Asians, where most men and very few women had slept rough. In group discussions those few who had slept rough had done so for only short periods of time, generally for a few nights until they found alternative accommodation. It was not considered a way of life.

> I got stranded in Bradford and spent one night on the train station. (Male resident, Hostel 3)

> I've slept in a train before because I stole something from Tesco and I thought I was going to get beaten if I went home. (Male resident, Hostel 3)

> … It happened to me. It was not through any circumstances to me … I was forced out and I had to live it rough for about three days. I couldn't take it any longer than that it was too cold … basically I found this old house and that gave me shelter. (Male resident, Hostel 1)

> As far as I'm concerned I've been living rough until I get my own place … even when I've lived with my friends … I would therefore say I have been living rough for four or five years now. (Male resident, Hostel 1)

> I was in Liverpool, I had only been there a couple of days. It's a funny thing because I was brought up in Liverpool as well. I went back ten years later and couldn't find anybody, so I was stuck. I had a brother who used to live there and I tried to find him but I couldn't … The reason I had to sleep in the street that night was because the alternative was the YMCA. I didn't want that so I was told to go and sleep in the street then. (Female resident, Hostel 2)

When asked why they would not sleep rough, the most common reply was that it was a matter of self-pride, although fear of harassment and physical violence was also mentioned.

> The streets are getting rougher, lots of stabbing and knives – no way. (Female resident, Hostel 3)

It should be noted, however, that the differences in rough sleeping across ethnic groups are not absolute – nearly half of young black men had slept rough, albeit often for short periods.

Experiencing hostels

Of those black young people who had stayed in a mainstream white-run hostel, many had negative experiences and were often referred to a black-run hostel after a short time.

> I was in a white hostel and did not like it. There was one black worker there who was working there temporarily and he said he knew somewhere else. He took on my case and he managed to get me out of there. They [white workers] weren't really trying to help me. (Male resident, Hostel 1)

> I went to a white women's hostel and I hated it there. I want to live with black people, there was no help for me there. (Female resident, Hostel 1)

> I used to live in that big dirty place [Shaftesbury House, Leeds] ... out of 200 people there were only two black people in there and there was pure racism in there. Some people even wanted to kill me – but I survived. (Male resident, Hostel 1)

> I've been in that one just round the corner and it's dirty with mould and everything, it's horrible ... there's no staff living there and people have just mashed it up. (Female resident, Hostel 3)

All of the respondents in all of the group discussions expressed a preference for black-run hostels.

> It's just different – it wouldn't bother me if these were all white residents and staff for a little while, but it would be different, I'd be less happy. (Female resident, Hostel 2)

> There needs to be black housing and hostels [everyone nods in agreement]. We are not racist, but we don't fit in with the white hostels, they can't identify with us. All they can do is be nice and say we understand, but they don't understand, because they are not like us. (Male resident, Hostel 1)

> I'm not racist, but until we are old enough to decide for ourselves, you cannot mix the two [colours] not until you have a strong identity of who you are. (Male resident, Hostel 1)

> It's been a life-saver. We black people do need somewhere that we as black people can feel safe. (Female resident, Hostel 2)

> If it was a white hostel I would feel unsafe as they [white people] go on as if they know what it is like to be black, but they don't really. You can see it in their faces, they don't like black people. But the staff here they want us to prosper and that makes them more caring towards us. (Female resident, Hostel 3)

For many, just being in a situation where all the residents and staff members were black was perceived to be positive, for others the fact that they were able to talk openly and freely to someone whom they felt really understood their particular situation was of most importance and they felt they could only get this level of support from black staff. There was a general feeling that only black staff genuinely wanted to help and that they tended to be more supportive than white staff.

> The staff are really nice and we are on first name basis here. If you want help, they will actually go with you and they will take you somewhere – they'll go out of their way for you. (Female resident, Hostel 1)

> I like the staff here. (Female resident, Hostel 2)

> We learn independence here and that's a good thing. Now when I get my own flat, I'm sorted. (Male resident, Hostel 3)

Locational choices

There were different locational preferences expressed with regard to both hostel provision and move-on accommodation. Some preferred to stay within their own communities, some felt that negative stereotyping of particular areas had disadvantaged them and they wished to 'move-out' to other areas, others sought refuge from their communities and anonymity in a different city in order to build a new life.

> I was born in this street and I like it because I am surrounded by everyone I know. I like it because it is in the heart of ———————. (Male resident, Hostel 1)

> I want to stay in ——————— because there are police everywhere you go and there is pure racism and aggravation elsewhere. (Male resident, Hostel 1)

> This area is getting bad. It doesn't matter what colour you are these days, it's just a crime-related area, you can't escape it. Basically what you work and live for you want it to be safe – that's all. (Female resident, Hostel 1)

Some of us want to move from the front-line but remain on the fringes of the inner city. (Male resident, Hostel 3)

I like it because its quiet, out of the ghetto and its got a good bus service. (Female resident, Hostel 1)

I like it here better than on the front-line because I would not be able to sleep up there. It's not comfortable and people just cause too much trouble up there. (Female resident, Hostel 1)

I want to go where nobody knows me. (Female resident, Hostel 1)

Moving on

Most young people were looking for self-contained accommodation provided by either the local authority or a housing association. Many criticised the nature of hostel provision because they had to share rooms and facilities. Most young people stressed that once they had their own accommodation, they would prefer to live alone.

It takes a certain amount of dignity or strength to live around others ... From being 15 years of age, I always wanted my own place ... When you live with others there's always agreements going on ... it's like have you finished in the shower yet or how come you've not washed out the bath ... I just want to be independent, see. (Male resident, Hostel 1)

Support needs

Young people generally expressed few concerns about moving into their own accommodation. Concerns ranged from feelings of responsibility and fear of not being able to cope, to concerns about managing financially and being burgled. However, on the whole very few people felt that they would need emotional or practical support.

I do get depressed sometimes so when I leave here I will need some help – it's just like leaving home all over again. (Female resident, Hostel 2)

At the moment I'm not ready to move on and there's no pressure here for me to. (Female resident, Hostel 2)

I was here about one and a half years ago and I kept worrying about bills, bills, bills and basic responsibilities that I did not have living here in the hostel. (Male resident, Hostel 1)

As long as I've got my music and TV I'll be OK. (Male resident, Hostel 3)

Hostel staff, questioned separately, did express concern for the young people and frequently remarked that problems really started once the young person was in permanent accommodation and that hostels were beginning to see young people return to them within a short space of time of them moving on. The reason given was the general lack of move-on support for young people and increasing financial problems.

> The problems start when they have moved into their own accommodation. We have not got the staff resources to do follow-up work and as a result they are left very much on their own. We are beginning to see people return because their tenancy had failed. (Staff member: black-run hostel, West Yorkshire)

The research team came increasingly to see this as at least in part a response to the family breakdown which had precipitated the young people's homelessness. Having left a family or household – or having been forced to – many respondents were reluctant to acknowledge that they may find it difficult to assume responsibility for running a home of their own. Very few resources, however, were available to support those who had moved on and the agency staff were acutely aware of the difficulties this created for many of their former residents.

Future aspirations

Generally, the young black people who took part in the group discussions had positive attitudes regarding their future. Many felt that once their housing situation had been sorted out, they would be able to resume further studies – a better education was thought to be the way to a better way of life by all interviewed. Many black males felt that their pre-16 education had seriously failed them, but were all the more determined to resume study.

> I went to some all-white school and I was discouraged from taking exams – they did not like me there. (Male resident, Hostel 1)

> I've learned more out on the streets than at school. School held me back and let me down. (Male resident, Hostel 1)

> The education many black people received was felt to be of little importance to them in future years in helping them to live in the real world. (Male resident, Hostel 1)

> They teach you maths, but they don't teach you how to spend money. (Female resident, Hostel 1)

> I want to get my qualifications. (Male resident, Hostel 1)

I want to be a writer, I hope to become a writer. (Male resident, Hostel 1)

Education was seen as very important to black men and women and was seen as the best way of 'making something of myself'. As one group member succinctly put it:

> Black people need education – not street mentality. We need more black people in the professions. We as a race were not brought up on violence. We don't need to act out what white people say we are. (Female resident, Hostel 1)

Summary of findings from the Discounted Voices study (Davies *et al.*, 1996)

E People from black and minority ethnic communities are disproportionately represented amongst those most vulnerable to homelessness, and *the problems faced by young homeless people from those communities are particularly serious.*

E *Young black minority ethnic homeless people showed a strong preference for black-led hostel accommodation,* as a step to their own rented accommodation, *but this provision was relatively scarce.*

E *The most common cause of homelessness among young people from all ethnic groups is a breakdown in personal relationships within the household.* Once the young person left the household, often into temporary accommodation, this was frequently followed by a subsequent improvement in family relationships. Other main causes of homelessness included fleeing physical or sexual violence (this was particularly significant for African-Caribbean and Asian young women), leaving care or penal institutions and eviction from insecure accommodation.

E *The experience of homelessness was both diverse and common across ethnic groups.* The majority of white young people had slept rough, whereas young African-Caribbeans and Asians were more likely to have stayed with friends and/or relatives. White homeless were most likely to turn to statutory and voluntary agencies for support, African-Caribbean homeless were less likely and Asian homeless least of all. Across ethnic groups, women were generally homeless for shorter periods of time than men.

E Few perceived the need for or received advice about maintaining an independent household. *Failure to maintain tenancies and lack of move-on support were causes for concern.*

E *A number of positive features were evident amongst black minority ethnic homeless which was reflected in a more generally optimistic outlook.* Most reported good physical and mental health, had high educational aspirations and saw themselves as being on the path to independent living.

Conclusions

Concern amongst local black and minority ethnic communities around the country at the level of young black homelessness was one of the key driving forces for the establishment of black-led housing projects and in the formation of the first black housing associations. The need to sustain, advocate and elaborate this social concern is equally important today. Overall, relationship conflicts within domestic households, abuse and violence of young people and life in forms of institutional care led to homelessness amongst our sample of respondents. These experiences were exacerbated by poverty, influenced by issues of gender and sexuality and embedded in differing cultural contexts. In this sense, becoming homeless was at the same time a similar and a different process across ethnic groups. The immediate aspects of homelessness include a combination of low income and lack of available housing to rent. The higher proportion of minority ethnic groups leaving care, unemployed and on low incomes, living in stressful overcrowded conditions and facing racial discrimination when seeking access to rented accommodation are likely to reproduce a persistent level of homelessness amongst these groups.

Homelessness amongst young people from black minority ethnic communities is a serious problem. The deficiencies of the data make it impossible to give a precise figure for its extent, or to determine trends in detail. What can be said is that the factors which exacerbate the problem amongst the black communities are growing and that there is no reason to believe that the existing provision is in any way adequate to meet the needs of this group of homeless people.

There are few hostels which conform to the ideal type identified by the respondents. It is scarcely surprising, therefore, that those which do exist are under extreme pressure. The exception to this is the relative shortfall of referrals of young black homeless women and this will require careful analysis. One obvious factor is the recent increase in provision in some cities. Another is that many homeless black women are fleeing domestic violence and have children. In such circumstances they may be more likely to stay in a refuge than the hostels studied here. It is also suggested, however, that the dislike of communal living and preference for staying with friends and relatives is particularly marked amongst this group.

There is a substantial gulf between young Asian homeless and the statutory and voluntary services. Low levels of demand and low levels of provision indicate that this gulf is unlikely to change without intervention. The need for advice, support, counselling, hostel provision and other forms of accommodation is clearly evident amongst Asian groups and likely to increase given their younger age structure. Attention to ethnic diversity in service provision by statutory and voluntary agencies, greater use of informal community-based networks and resourcing Asian-led provision will all assist in breaking down this divide.

There is also a clear and pressing need and demand for more general black-led hostels. At the same time, there is also a need to integrate those hostels within a broad range of provision. As other studies have demonstrated, the diverse needs of single homeless people require the provision of a wide range of accommodation; including direct access, medium stay, special needs hostels and different forms of move-on. There also needs to be machinery for coordinating all of this. It is essential that black-led projects are fully integrated into this provision and not seen as 'specialist' or marginal to it.

The sensitive issue of support for move-on needs to be faced. Further research is required to explore how far the present emphasis upon the provision of independent accommodation is the appropriate goal, and to determine what packages of help and support would be most acceptable to young people who do move and most effective in aiding them to settle in their new homes and reduce the level of failed tenancies. Even at this point, however, the evidence of the agency survey and of other studies would suggests strongly that more resources must be found for move-on support.

Last, there are persistent problems in data collection that may inhibit policy intervention. The inadequacy of local authority ethnic monitoring of homeless applications is of major concern. Despite the decades of attention to this issue, most local authorities could not adequately assess the demand from black and minority ethnic young single homeless. This position is both reflected and encouraged by the failure to include specification of such data in the DoE's P1E return. The National Federation of Housing Associations Core data system does permit special tabulation of ethnicity by homeless by age, and collection of national data from hostels in a similar way would provide a particularly useful data archive.

References

Amin, K. (1996) 'Young people and unemployment.' *Runnymede Trust Bulletin*, February.

Anderson, I., Kemp, P. and Quilgars, D. (1993) *Single Homeless People.* London: HMSO.

Braham, P., Rattansi, A. and Skellington, R. (eds) *Racism and Antiracism: Inequalities, Opportunities and Policies.* London: Sage/Open University.

Campbell and Devore Associates Ltd (1990) Report on the Pagnell Street Hostel, Lewisham. Unpublished, Resettlement Unit.

ChildLine (1996) *Children and Racism: A ChildLine Study.* London: M. Macleod.

Coles, B. and Craine, S. (1995) 'Alternative careers: young transitions and young people's involvement in crime.' *Youth and Policy 48*, Spring.

Commission For Racial Equality (1983) *Collingwood Housing Association Ltd, Report of a Formal Investigation.* London: CRE.

Commission For Racial Equality (1984a) *Race and Housing in Liverpool, A Research Report.* London: CRE.

Commission For Racial Equality (1984b) *Race and Council Housing in Hackney.* London: CRE.

Commission For Racial Equality (1985) *Race and Mortgage Lending.* London: CRE.

Commission For Racial Equality (1988a) *Racial Discrimination in a London Estate Agency: Report of a Formal Investigation into Richard Barclay and Co.* London: CRE.

Commission For Racial Equality (1988b) *Homelessness and Discrimination: Report into the London Borough of Tower Hamlets.* London: CRE.

Commission For Racial Equality (1989a) *Racial Discrimination in an Oldham Estate Agency: Report of a Formal Investigation into Norman Lester and Co.* London: CRE.

Commission For Racial Equality (1989b) *Racial Discrimination in Liverpool City Council: Report of a Formal Investigation into the Housing Department.* London: CRE.

Commission For Racial Equality (1989c) *Racial Discrimination in Property Development: Report of a Formal Investigation into Oaklawn Developments Ltd, Leicestershire.* London: CRE.

Commission For Racial Equality (1989d) *Race Relations Act 1976, A Guide for Accommodation Bureaux, Landladies and Landlords.* London: CRE.

Commission For Racial Equality (1990a) *'Sorry It's Gone': Testing For Racial Discrimination in the Private Rented Sector.* London: CRE.

Commission For Racial Equality (1990b) *Code of Practice in Non-Rented (Owner-Occupied) Housing, Consultation Draft.* London: CRE.

Commission For Racial Equality (1990c) *Out of Order: Report of a Formal Investigation into the London Borough of Southwark.* London: CRE.

Commission For Racial Equality (1991) *Code of Practice in Rented Housing.* London: CRE.

Commission For Racial Equality (1992) *Racial Discrimination in Hostel Accommodation: Report of a Formal Investigation of Refugee Housing Association Ltd.* London: CRE.

Commission For Racial Equality (1993a) *Housing Associations and Racial Equality in Scotland: Report of a Formal Investigation.* London: CRE.

Commission For Racial Equality (1993b) *Housing Associations and Racial Equality: Report of a Formal Investigation into Housing Associations in Wales, Scotland and England.* London: CRE.

Commission For Racial Equality (1993c) *Room for All: Tenant's Associations and Racial Equality.* London: CRE.

Community Relations Commission (1974) *Unemployment and Homelessness.* London: CRE.

Davies, J. and Lyle, S., with Deacon, A., Law, I., Julienne, L. and Kay, H. (1996) *Discounted Voices, Homelessness Amongst Young Black and Minority Ethnic People in England.* Sociology and Social Policy Working Paper 15, School of Sociology and Social Policy, University of Leeds.

Elam, G. (1992) *Survey of Admissions to London Resettlement Units.* London: HMSO.

Ginsburg, N. (1992) 'Racism and housing: concepts and reality.' In P. Braham, A. Rattansi and R. Skellington (eds) *Racism and Antiracism: Inequalities, Opportunities and Policies.* London: Sage/Open University.

Green, A.E. (1994) *The Geography of Poverty and Wealth: Evidence on the Changing Spatial Distribution and Segregation of Poverty and Wealth from the Census of Population 1991 and 1981.* Warwick: Institute for Employment Research.

Hagell, A. and Shaw, C. (1996) *Opportunity and Disadvantage at Age 16; a Report of a Major Survey of Over 3,000 16 Year Olds from 34 Schools in English Inner Cities.* London: Policy Studies Institute.

Harrison, M. (1995) *Housing, 'Race' and Empowerment.* Aldershot: Centre for Research in Ethnic Relations/Avebury.

Hills, J. (1995) *Inquiry into Income and Wealth, Volumes 1 and 2.* York: Joseph Rowntree Foundation.

Joseph Rowntree Foundation (1995) *Inquiry into Income and Wealth.* York: Joseph Rowntree Foundation.

Law, I. (1996) *Racism, Ethnicity and Social Policy.* Hemel Hempstead: Prentice Hall/Harvester Wheatsheaf.

Moore, J., Canter, D., Stockley, D. and Drake, M. (1991) *Faces of Homelessness: Summary.* Surrey: University of Surrey.

Randall, G. (1994) *Counted Out.* London: Crisis and CHAR.

Randall, G. and Brown, S. (1993) *The Rough Sleepers Initiative: An Evaluation.* London: HMSO.

Sarre, P., Phillips, D. and Skellington, R. (1989) *Ethnic Minority Housing: Explanations and Policies.* Aldershot: Avebury.

Scott, J. (1991) A Survey of Female Users of Resettlement Units. Unpublished, Department of Social Security.

Smith, J. and Gilford, S., (1993) *Birmingham Young People in Housing Need Project.* Ilford: Barnardo's.

Smith, S.J. with Hill, S. (1991) *'Race' and Housing in Britain, a Review and Research Agenda.* Edinburgh: University of Edinburgh.

Strathdee, R. (1993) *Housing Our Children.* London: Centrepoint.

TUC (1995) *Black and Betrayed: a Report on Black Workers' Experience of Unemployment and Low Pay in 1994–95*. London: TVC.

TUC (1996) *Underworked and Underpaid: a Report on Young People's Labour Market Experiences in the 1990s*. London: TUC.

Wilkinson, H. and Mulgan, G. (1996) *Freedom's Children: Work, Relationships and Politics for 18–34 Year Olds in Britain Today*. London: DEMOS.

Ye-Myint, C. (1992) *Who's Hiding?* No Fixed Abode.

Further reading

Anderson, I. (1993) *Access to Housing for Low Income Single Homeless People: A Review of Research and Policy Issues*. York: University of York.

Bannister, J. *et al.*, (1993) *Homeless Young People in Scotland*. London: HMSO.

Barnado's/Ujima Housing Association (1991) *Young, Black and Homeless in London*. Ilford: Barnardo's.

Craig, G. (1991) *Fit For Nothing?* London: Children's Society.

Dalton, M. and Daghlian, S. (1989) *Race and Housing in Glasgow: The Role of Housing Associations*. London: CRE.

Ford, J. and Vincent, J. (1990) *Homelessness Amongst Afro-Caribbean Women in Leicester*. Leicester: Foundation Housing Association Ltd.

Garside, P., Grimshaw, R. and Ward, F. (1990) *No Place Like Home: The Hostels Experience*. London: Department of the Environment.

Greve, J. and Currie, E. (1990) *Homelessness in Britain*. York: Joseph Rowntree Foundation.

Hendessi, M. (1987) *Migrants: The Invisible Homeless*. London: Migrant Services Unit.

Hendessi, M. (1992) *4 In 10*. London: CHAR.

Ivegbuma, J. (1989) 'Local authorities and black single homelessness.' *Black Housing 5*, 5.

Jones, T. (1993) *Britain's Ethnic Minorities*. London: Policy Studies Institute.

Julienne, L. (1994) 'The housing corporation's black housing strategy review.' *Black Housing*, May/June, 13–16.

Law, I., Harrison, M. and Phillips, D. (1995) *Equity and Difference: Racial and Ethnic Inequalities in Housing Needs and Housing Investment in Leeds*. Leeds: School of Sociology and Social Policy Research Report, University of Leeds.

Leigh, C. (1993) *Right to Care*. London: CHAR.

London Against Racism in Housing (1988) *Anti-Racism and the Private Sector*. London.

Mirrlees-Black, C. and Aye Maung, N. (1994) *Fear of Crime: Findings from the 1992 British Crime Survey*. London: Home Office Research and Statistics Department.

Mullings, B. (1991) *The Colour of Money: The Impact of Housing Investment Decision Making on Black Housing Outcomes in London*. London: London Race and Housing Research Unit.

Owen, D. (1992) *Ethnic Minorities in Great Britain: Settlement Patterns, 1991 Census Statistical Paper No.1*. Warwick: Centre for Research in Ethnic Relations, University of Warwick.

Owen, D. (1993) *Ethnic Minorities in Great Britain: Housing and Family Characteristics, 1991 Census Statistical Paper No.4.* Warwick: Centre for Research in Ethnic Relations, University of Warwick.

Peach, C. and Byron M. (1993) 'Caribbean tenants in council housing: "race", class and gender.' *New Community 19*, 3.

Smith, S.J. (1989) *The Politics of 'Race' and Residence.* Oxford: Polity Press.

Strathdee, R. (1992) *No Way Back.* London: Centrepoint.

Virdee, S. (1995) *Racial Violence and Harassment.* London: Policy Studies Institute.

Webster, C. (1995) *Youth Crime, Victimisation and Racial Harassment.* Paper in Community Studies, Bradford: Bradford and Ilkley Community College.

CHAPTER 7

Can Owner-Occupation Take the Strain?

Janet Ford

Introduction

The expansion of owner-occupation has been a constant feature of housing policy for a number of decades and there is little evidence from either of the main political parties that this emphasis is likely to change in the foreseeable future. The Labour government elected in May 1997 is virtually indistinguishable from previous Conservative administrations in its support for owner-occupation.

Currently, 67 per cent of all households are owner-occupiers; a concentration unknown in most other European countries. The recent and current mechanisms used to implement this policy are varied, and include financial deregulation, right to buy, rents to mortgages, do-it-yourself shared ownership (DIYSO), other forms of low-cost home ownership and tenants incentive schemes. Voluntary Purchase Grants are the latest, if not very promising, device. Until very recently, local authority receipts from the sale of rental property were ring fenced, and new-build programmes limited. The financial regime applied to social housing has limited the impact of that sector in terms of the number of new housing units provided. The private rented sector remains small. Housing choice has been eroded relatively quickly and restrictions on tenure choice has contributed to social and economic polarisation (Lee *et al.*, 1995; Burrows, 1997).

This paper will argue that current housing policy and the tenure emphasis it has created is in urgent need of reconsideration and modification. The argument could be made in terms of the principle of choice, and the absence of choice with respect to tenure for many people is regrettable. But the argument can also be made in terms of the appropriateness of the current tenure system in the light of the current direction of social and economic change. Structural change is impacting on both owner-occupation and social housing. The implication of these changes for both sectors are substantial and while they are different they are nevertheless interrelated.

There are a number of key structural changes taking place in Britain; demographic changes in labour market opportunities, changes to household structures and in the privatisation of welfare. This paper can obviously only make a start in discussing the nature of social and economic change in contemporary Britain and its impact on the housing system. Consequently, just one form of change, that of labour market change, will be considered here, and used as an exemplar of contemporary change. First, I want to consider some key aspects of labour market change, second to identify some of its implications for home ownership, and third, some of its implications for social housing. The extent of which changes suggest the need for some modification in current policy responses will then be considered.

A changing structure of labour market opportunities

The broad contours of the recent and predicted changes to the labour market are well understood and documented. Employment grew between 1981 and 1995 by 1.4 million. Between now and 2001 around a further million jobs are expected to be available, bringing predicted total employment to 26.2 million. The nature of these jobs is, however, changing and the main changes are summarised below.

- E Service sector jobs will increase by 1.3 million.

- E Manufacturing jobs will continue to fall, and a further 200,000 will be lost.

- E As a percentage of all jobs there will be fewer full-time jobs.

- E Part-time jobs will increase, probably by around a further 1.3 million.

- E Self-employment is likely to increase by 440,000.

In addition, more of these jobs, whether full-time or part-time, will be temporary and/or casual and fixed-term contracts will continue to grow.

These changes are illustrative of the range of issues that need to be explored, focusing on their extent and nature and likely impact in more detail. Below, four aspects of these changes are considered: temporary employment; employment durations; higher unemployment and low-wage employment.

These are all potentially important areas of development because their growth will result in greater uncertainty for individuals and households, through one or more of a growing number of job changes, an increased likelihood of more spells of unemployment and fluctuating and often lower income from work.

Temporary employment

Labour market researchers have been predicting for a considerable time now that the competitive and deregulated labour market would result in more temporary working (Atkinson and Meagher, 1986). To varying degrees writers suggested that organisations in a highly competitive environment, particularly facing unpredictable markets, would opt for a core of permanent workers and exploit the opportunities for temporary workers to meet fluctuating demand for their goods or services, and so reduce the permanent costs borne by the organisation. For some time it looked as though these predictions were unlikely to be fulfilled, or more limited in their impact, but since the early 1990s the upward trend in the use of temporary workers has been clear, as can be seen in Figure 7.1.

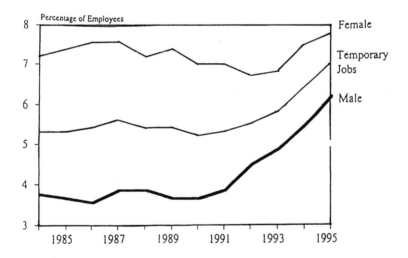

Figure 7.1 Temporary employment in the UK, 1984–1995
Source: Labour Force Survey (Spring quarters)

It is also interesting to note that temporary employment is increasing across all sectors of industry and commerce (Beatson, 1995). Larger firms make the greatest use of temporary workers and the reasons for their use are also changing. For a long time, temporary workers were used to cover events such as holidays and maternity leave, but now their use is for more routine staffing arrangements whereby a minimum core of permanent workers are supplemented by 'on-call' temporary workers as they are needed. This pattern is now well developed in the financial services sector and in service companies like British Telecom, retailing companies, and in 'term-time only' contracts in the provision of some educational services.

Employment durations

As the employment structure changes, there is also evidence that the duration of many permanent jobs is shortening (Gregg and Wadsworth, 1995). This is a significant change because despite the growth of temporary, casual work, the majority of those in employment still have 'permanent' jobs. Again, there is a debate about how significant a change in employment durations is taking place, but two things are well documented.

- E For any one of the main forms of 'permanent' employment, the trend with respect to average duration is a downward one.

- E The kinds of employment opportunities that are predicted to grow in the future (for example, part-time or self-employment) are those with the shorter rather than longer durations.

Figure 7.2 indicates the average changes in several different forms of employment since 1975.

Researchers have also shown the interaction between the changing pattern of employment and the distribution of men and women in the labour market. As a consequence, for men, overall, average employment durations are falling while for women, on average, employment durations are rising, although still lagging behind those of men. While all these changes are gradual, and the majority of people still have longer term, permanent employment, the trend towards shorter duration jobs and an increasing number of jobs over one's working life, sometimes interspersed with periods of unemployment, is now well established.

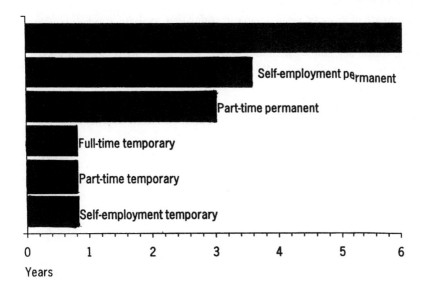

Figure 7.2 Employment durations, (1992)
Source: Gregg and Wadsworth, 1995

Higher unemployment

The persistence of high levels of unemployment is also an important structural change in the labour market. While unemployment is clearly influenced by cyclical change, the current situation where around two million registered claimants characterise the top of the economic cycle is a substantial change. There are significant differences in the unemployment rates experienced by men and women, and between groups such as renters and owner-occupiers, but, in terms of the concerns of this paper, it is interesting to note that whereas home owners used to have negligible risk of unemployment, by 1993 (the recent peak year), approximately 5 per cent of mortgagors had lost employment and were unemployed. This reflected both the changing composition of mortgagors, but also that professional and managerial occupations now carry some risk.

Low wage employment

The growth of low paid work is also something that needs to be noted. Those forms of employment predicted to grow most strongly – part-time employment, temporary employment and self-employment – are often associated with low wage employment. While average incomes rise, the pool of low paid workers has grown, and now exceeds 10 million workers if part-time pro rata workers are included. Low paid work has often been seen as an issue of female employment, and indeed it is, but interestingly, recent work has shown the extent to which men and particularly those in mid-career are now in low paid work. Table 7.1 indicates the trend in the distribution of low pay between men and women in full-time employment for the period 1982 to 1996.

Table 7.1 Full-time employees with gross weekly earnings below the Council of Europe's decency threshold (£239.16 per week in 1996)

	1982	*1988*	*1991*	*1992*	*1993*	*1994*	*1996*
				millions			
Women	2.75	2.91	2.92	2.8	2.72	2.71	2.73
Men	1.83	2.77	2.81	2.97	2.73	2.76	2.88
All	4.58	5.68	5.72	5.77	5.45	5.47	5.61

Source: Derived from the *New Earnings Survey* by the Low Pay Unit
Note: Earnings are for all workers on adult rates, excluding overtime

Finally, one way of demonstrating that the changes discussed above are significant changes is to look at the types of jobs currently on offer in the labour market, i.e. at the change 'at the margin'. Recent analyses of vacancy data shows that around 30 per cent of vacancies filled are for full-time jobs, 33 per cent are part-time and 20 per cent for self-employed posts. This balance differs from the current stock of jobs where approximately 60 per cent are full-time jobs, 12 per cent self-employed and 28 per cent part-time. The processes restructuring the stock of jobs are clear and underway. While it will take time before the shift is noticeable in the stock of jobs, the likely direction of change in the employment characteristics of households is also clear. Thus, structural labour market change is quite well rooted. These developments raise the question of their implications for and impact on

housing in general and on those in different tenure positions in particular.
The implications of these structural changes may well differ with respect to
owner-occupation and social housing and each will be considered separately
below.

Labour market changes and owner-occupation

There is already evidence of the impact of labour market change on
owner-occupation in the form of changes in economic characteristics of
those buying property with a mortgage. Table 7.2 compares the
characteristics of mortgagors in 1981 with those in 1995/96.

Table 7.2 Employment status of mortgagor heads
of household, 1981–1995/96

Year	Full-time	Part-time	U/Ed	Retired	Disabled /sick	Economic inactive	Total
1981	92	1	3	2	1	1	100
1984	90	2	3	2	1	2	100
1988	88	2	3	3	1	2	100
1991	86	3	4	4	2	2	100
1995/ 96	84	4	3	4	3	2	100

Source: Derived from the housing trailers to the Labour Force Survey, 1981–1993;
  SEH, 1995/96

Since 1981, there has been a reduction in the proportion of mortgagors who
are in full-time employment so that by 1995/96 just over four-fifths were in
this position. In terms of the number of households affected, roughly 1.7
million mortgagors lacked full-time employment in 1995 compared with
under 500,000 in 1981. In 1995/96 some of these 1.7 million mortgagors
were in part-time work (420,000) but the vast majority were either
unemployed, retired, disabled or economically inactive, potentially with
limited income, yet responsible for mortgage payments.

Amongst mortgagors in full-time employment, approximately 20 per cent
are self-employed (Ford, Kempson and Wilson, 1995). Thus, one-fifth of
owner-occupiers have a labour market position where average durations of

employment are relatively low (three years). Self-employment is also precarious because of the high failure rate amongst small businesses (estimates suggest that one in three fail in the first three years). It is also often poorly paid while it lasts. Of 1.6 million self-employed mortgagor heads of household in 1994, over 40 per cent were households with below half average incomes (before housing costs). Self-employment is also expected to reach 3.7 million by 2001. The very attraction of 'an asset' against which business borrowing can be secured encourages self-employment amongst mortgagors. Further, one of the difficult things for lenders is that a proportion of borrowers who start their mortgagors as employees 'convert' themselves to self-employed status without notification, particularly after unemployment or redundancy.

Drawing this evidence together, indicative estimates show that just under a one-third of mortgagors are currently either in the most precarious forms of employment or not in employment at all.

The risk of unemployment

Despite the trends outlined above, unemployment amongst mortgagors remains low, at the height of the recession it was no more than 5 per cent overall compared with a national rate that exceeded 10 per cent, and an average tenant rate of over 15 per cent. If we look at what happens over a year – the unemployed flow – then 6 per cent of mortgagors experience unemployment in any one year, again a lower incidence than amongst tenants. In addition, the trends outlined above suggest that owner-occupiers may well continue to experience unemployment at least at the current levels of 3 per cent (1995) and that there will be an upwards pressure. In part this is due to the drawing into owner-occupation of households from the lower socio-economic groups with their higher risk of unemployment. But also, as more owners from any group find themselves in more precarious jobs, the risk of at least spells of unemployment will increase.

So there is evidence that structural change in the labour market has begun to affect the characteristics of the owner-occupied sector. The question is, does it matter?

The impact of labour market change on owner-occupation: does it matter?

All these changes outlined above have the potential to challenge people's ability to manage owner-occupation and to warrant caution on the part of mortgage lenders. But is there any evidence that this potential is being realised; are the changes in fact problematic? There is still a public (state) safety net, even if its action is delayed as has been the case since October 1995 when further restrictions on income support mortgage interest (ISMI) were introduced. Borrowers often have savings and other resources, and more frequent job changes need not mean unemployment. In any case, for most people periods of unemployment are short; *job instability* is not necessarily incompatible with *employment stability*.

In practice, there is evidence that the structural change outlined above has real consequences for owner-occupiers and lenders. As Mike Blackburn noted in his paper in this volume, 'We cannot disguise the fact that these changes in the job market alter the nature of risk and the process of risk assessment. We will be more cautious and so will potential borrowers.' This may result in the terms and conditions for entry to home ownership tightening in particular instances (higher deposits, lower income to loan ratios etc.), excluding some would-be borrowers. These changes may well be at the margins of lending, and not all lenders will respond in the same way, although it is likely that it will always be possible to find the 100 per cent mortgage at a price. But already there is documented evidence of some lenders raising their threshold credit scores and rejecting more applicants and widespread evidence that applicants who are self-employed are having the lending rules applied far more rigorously than has been the case for a decade or more (Ford and Kempson, 1997). Employment histories are now explored seriously by most lenders. Inevitably, directly or indirectly, more people will fail to qualify for loans. This caution on the part of both households and lenders will slow or reverse the trend towards increasing numbers of precarious workers within the sector. So it is likely that in the next year's Survey of English Housing we might see an increase in the number of mortgagors who are in full-time work. This will not be due to better labour market opportunities, but to lenders adopting more risk averse policies. Some borrowers may equally be more cautious.

Any growth in risk averse behaviour is likely to increase the demand for social housing and private renting. But where high risk applicants do gain acceptance to owner-occupation (perhaps through the return of fringe lending), the risks to them of payments problems will be high. But in addition, even amongst relatively cautious borrowers, greater risk and so potentially payment difficulties are likely to be encountered by a proportion of borrowers.

Payment problems

Over the three years January 1991–January 1994, the period of the recent recession, around one-fifth of all mortgagors reported some difficulty in meeting their mortgage payments. A smaller proportion actually defaulted, and while, since the height of the recession, the number has fallen, the important point is that two recent government surveys, 1994/95 and 1995/96 Surveys of English Housing, show a continuingly stubborn proportion of mortgagors with payment difficulties. Both surveys are post-recession surveys, so likely to be picking up structural rather than cyclical factors. The surveys show that this is in fact the case, with difficulties overwhelmingly attributed to changes in the form of labour market opportunity and experiences (rather than unemployment), which under-mines the capacity of borrowers to sustain the prerequisites of owner-occupation. Failed self-employment and loss of earnings due to re-employment at a lower wage following unemployment or an alteration in the pay and conditions of the same job are amongst the most frequently cited reasons for payment difficulties (Burrows and Ford, 1998; Ford *et al.*, 1995).

Social housing and social and economic change

Economic change in the form of labour market restructuring affects social housing in at least three ways:

E   by social housing accommodating those owner-occupiers who lose their homes as a result of arrears; arrears which are caused in large part by labour market difficulties

E   by social housing tenants bearing the brunt of job loss, unemployment and low paid work

E   through social housing tenants experiencing the brunt of the impact of the work disincentives.

Accommodating the fallout from owner-occupation

Of the 350,000 households moving out of owner-occupation since 1990 as a result of payment difficulties, by early 1996, 70 per cent (240,000) have so far been rehoused in social housing. Overwhelmingly these are households with dependent children, and overwhelmingly they are households who now have no one at work. Many of them have outstanding debts, not just their mortgage lenders but often to other creditors and on household bills. Thus, one source of growing demand for social housing has come from those who could not now sustain owner-occupation, although they may of course do so again in the future. Access to social housing following repossession may be direct or indirect, depending on whether households present themselves on possession or only after a period of time with family and friends (Ford and Kempson, 1997), but given that possessions look to have reached a plateau of around 40,000 a year, demand for social housing following repossession is likely to continue.

Social housing and labour market restructuring

In the 1960s and 1970s social housing tenants had a mix of characteristics, often traditional manual and particularly skilled workers. Social housing tenants, however, have also borne the impact of labour market restructuring, in the form of the decline in primary and manufacturing employment. Since 1981, 1.3 million jobs have been lost in these sectors; skilled, semi-skilled and unskilled jobs. This ensured that unemployment amongst tenants was substantial. Many of those who lost their jobs in this way, if they were able to find work at all, could only do so in the emerging low wage sectors. For tenants, particularly men (often the main breadwinners in households) it can often be difficult to find work as most of the available jobs are in the part-time service sectors, traditionally regarded as 'women's jobs'. They are also typically low paid. Many average wages in service sector jobs are currently under £4 an hour. Many jobs advertised in the Employment Service pay between £2 and £3 an hour.

The problems created by unemployment, restructuring and a low wage economy for social housing providers and tenants are potentially severe. Together, these developments have played an important part in reducing and limiting the social and economic mix within social housing and add to the difficulties that social housing providers face in meeting their commitment to provide socially and economically mixed communities. Central to these changes are the ways in which individuals and households respond to these developments.

The response to this situation is varied. One response of tenants to unemployment, particularly amongst those who are older, but still of working age, is to withdraw from the labour market. This is particularly true of men. Their competitive position is weak and the rates of pay, if they could get a job, are sometimes regarded as an affront to skilled craftsmen. As a result there has been a marked increase in economic inactivity amongst tenants of working age (National Housing Federation, 1996).

A second possible response to unemployment is to take whatever work can be obtained and to rely on means-tested in-work benefits to boost income.

Work disincentives

The ability and willingness of tenants to take low wage employment is closely bound up with other aspects of housing and social security policy. In particular, with the policy of higher rents (if no longer indefinitely rising) and the use of housing benefit to assist low income tenants in and out of work with housing costs. The detail of these arrangements are well rehearsed (Ford and Wilcox, 1994; Ford, Kempson and England, 1996) and do not need to be repeated here. It is the current outcome of these relationships that is important. Two outcomes are central:

E First, the growth of low waged work alongside rising rents has drawn an increasing number of tenant households into the scope of benefit

E Second, the structure of in-work Housing Benefit creates a work disincentive. The structure of benefit is such that above a threshold it is withdrawn at a steep rate for every additional pound earned (the operation of the taper). This results in a situation where someone earning around £280 a week, with a £50 rent, will be little better off than someone earning £80 and with £50 rent. This *unemployment trap* is not much of an incentive to take employment and some people will therefore only accept work if they can be clear of benefit entirely.

Both of these responses to the changing labour market bring disadvantages. To the extent that people respond to these disincentive effects by not taking work, and either remain unemployed or become economically inactive, the social and economic mix of social housing is further eroded. And there are more people now facing such a choice. Equally, if people disregard these disincentives and work for no more than they might receive on benefit, or even less, they are clearly at risk of poverty and rent arrears. Both of these situations appear to be on the increase.

One of the areas of social housing activity where there is growing concern about these work disincentive effects is where housing associations are engaged in development and redevelopment work on estates, often local authority estates. Improved properties invariably carry a higher rent, but tenants being moved to them may have had no change in their incomes. They may face a situation where Housing Benefit will not cover all the additional rent and where they could be quite considerably worse off unless they have access to employment at higher wages. Recent anecdotal evidence of this process comes from some of the housing action trusts (HATs) where housing associations report that previously employed tenants are now either unemployed or looking for property at their previous rent level or closer to it. One possible response may be to seek a move into the lower rent local authority sector. A further implication is that higher rent areas are increasingly likely to house concentrations of unemployed households.

Policy issues

Structural change in the labour market, either on its own or in combination with other aspects of housing and social security policy, have real and visible effects for owner-occupation and social housing. The tensions between key structures and processes are marked and even if they do not worsen any further, they already raise important questions as to how the effects can be reversed or mitigated. What are the policy implications of these developments? Some suggestions follow.

Public policy responses

The clearest implication of the changes outlined is the need for additional housing outside the owner-occupier sector. This is now a familiar call, but no less important for that. Changing policy is sometimes a dripping tap exercise. Owner-occupation is probably at its limit around the 67 per cent mark (although not everyone subscribes to this view), although some expansion beyond this point is planned. Additional housing outside the sector is certainly required to allow households, and particularly younger households, to enter owner-occupation when they feel it is appropriate and not because they cannot find or gain access to alternative housing. There is plenty of evidence that the transition to adult independence is becoming prolonged, but in the meantime young people have to be housed. Parents cannot always be the source of this housing and private rented property can be scarce, expensive and of poor quality. Benefit restrictions introduced in October 1996 for the under-25s now make access to private rented accommodation less likely for young people and recently formed first households, many of whom are low-income households. Social housing becomes an even greater priority.

Another way of responding to the issue of the strain on owner-occupation is to consider increasing support to the sector. There are two kinds of support required. One is the development of an effective out-of-work safety net and the other is assistance to in-work low income owners. The state safety net (ISMI) is gradually being eroded and the provision of a private insurance safety net remains problematic.

The retreat by the state from support for many mortgagors, first eroded in 1987, was taken further in October 1995 when the expectation that mortgagors should cover themselves through the private insurance market became public policy. At that same time, no more than 16 per cent of borrowers had insurance. Today, take up is higher, but only about one in five borrowers are covered. Take-up is much higher amongst first-time buyers, but the 50 per cent of business that is introduced to lenders by intermediaries typically remains outside of the insurance net.

One of the early doubts concerned the extent to which the kinds of employment opportunities being created or extended by the structural changes in the labour market could be covered by private insurance; self-employment, temporary working, broken employment records and spells of unemployment. A recently completed evaluation of these changes indicates that many of the higher risk categories of workers (e.g. self-employed) who were previously excluded, are now more likely to be able to obtain a policy, but likely to have specific conditions attached to their policies that may exclude at the point of any claim (Ford and Kempson, 1997). Borrowers, however, face a number of deterrents to take-up of mortgage payments protection insurance (MPPI). These include its cost, a lack of knowledge amongst borrowers of the restrictions to the state safety net and the average 50 per cent of mortgage business that is introduced by intermediaries. Centrally, however, borrowers also have some very negative attitudes towards insurance and insurers *per se*, and this issue has to be addressed if take-up is likely to improve.

As a result of the influences outlined above, of the third of mortgagors at greatest risk of being unable to pay their mortgage payments in the event of losing all income, only one in four has MPPI. Should cyclical unemployment start to rise, or structurally generated job insecurity increase, higher arrears and possessions will follow.

The other form of support to owner-occupiers that would assist is some benefit akin to Housing Benefit, that is an in-work benefit for low-income mortgagors. This is the Mortgage Benefit debate, again well-rehearsed, widely endorsed and constantly rejected by government (Webb and Wilcox, 1991; Wilcox and Williams, 1996).

The issues of work disincentives and their impact on housing association tenant profiles might be approached in a number of ways. Anything that keeps rents down must help and there is some evidence of a retreat from full market rents and also changes in the criteria used to assess bids for funding to the Housing Corporation where rent levels and proposed increases are considered. Equally, anything that raises wages at the bottom end of the market is of positive benefit. The issues around a minimum wage are very actually important to tenants.

Structural change also raises some doubts about the targets set for the portfolio of provision, particularly amongst housing associations with respect to low cost home ownership as well as the likely success of measures designed to continue right to buy. While shared ownership has an important place in housing low income households, unless it can be 'staircased' up and down it may still prove difficult for some households. The need for rental accommodation meanwhile suffers.

Many of these policy prescriptions presume political will. The last Conservative government accorded little priority to housing, and as yet there is little sign of substantial policy innovation on the part of the Labour government, although perhaps some change of attitude and approach, particularly with regard to homelessness and capital receipts. However, the problems remain substantial, and as a result, if housing associations like St Anne's and others thought that they might be needed less in the future, that cannot be conceived of. But the context looks to be a difficult one.

References

Atkinson, J. and Meager, N. (1986) *Changing Working Patterns: How Companies Achieve Flexibility to Meet New Needs.* London: Nodo.

Beatson, M. (1995) *Labour Market Flexibility*, Research Report No. 48. London: Department of Employment.

Burrows, R. (1997) *Contemporary Patterns of Residential Mobility in Relation to Social Housing in England.* York: Centre for Housing Policy.

Burrows, R. and Ford, J. (1998) 'Self-employment and home ownership: after the enterprise culture.' *Work, Employment and Society 21, 1,* 97–119.

Ford, J. and Kempson, E. (1997) *Bridging the Gap? Safety-nets for Mortgage Borrowers.* York: Centre for Housing Policy.

Ford, J. and Wilcox, S. (1994) *Affordable Housing, Low Incomes and the Flexible Labour Market.* London: National Federation of Housing Associations.

Ford, J., Kempson, E. and England, J. (1996) *Into Work? The Impact of Housing Costs and Housing Benefits on the Decision to Work.* York: Joseph Rowntree Foundation.

Ford, J., Kempson, E. and Wilson, M. (1995) *Mortgage Arrears and Possessions: Perspectives from Borrowers, Lenders and the Courts.* London: HMSO.

Gregg, P. and Wadsworth, J. (1995) 'A short history of labour turnover, job tenure and job security, 1975–1993.' *Oxford Review of Economic Policy 11*, 1, 73–90.

Lee, P., Murie, A., Marsh, A. and Riseborough, M. (1995) *The Price of Social Exclusion.* London: National Federation of Housing Associations.

National Housing Federation (1996) *Annual Report of the CORE Data, 1995–96.* London: National Housing Federation.

Webb, S. and Wilcox, S. (1991) *Time for Mortgage Benefits.* York: Joseph Rowntree Foundation.

Wilcox, S. and Williams, P. (1996) *Coping with Mortgage Default: Lessons from the Recession.* London: Council of Mortgage Lenders.

CHAPTER 8

The Role of the Lender, 2000+
J.M. Blackburn

Introduction

I wish to discuss how we at the Halifax see our role as a lender – specifically
in the housing sector – in the next ten to twenty years. I suspect that the main
interests of most readers are in the future of the rented sector, but first I want
to set the scene. I will sketch out how we see UK population and households
in the next generation, and what we think about the further growth of
owner-occupation. Then I will examine social renting – mainly by local
authorities and housing associations – and the role private finance can play in
this sector. I will discuss ways in which the private renting sector could at
least be stabilised and perhaps even encouraged to play the part that it does in
other countries. Finally, I will consider briefly the Private Finance Initiative
and the opportunities it gives to improve the infrastructure and social fabric
of the country.

Housing: the background

Building societies were founded to help resolve a problem – that of urban
housing in the nineteenth century, inadequate in quantity and quality. They
were also formed to exploit an opportunity – higher industrial wages giving
people the chance to save and to buy their own homes. We still have major
problems in the UK housing, but we don't see the step change in the economy that we saw in the last century. The demographics, in particular are very
different. The population of the UK grew by 72 per cent between 1851 and
1901. This was accompanied by massive migration from the countryside to
the new industrial centres. Population grew again by 31 per cent between
1901 and 1951 with the major trend being the expansion of the new

suburbs. Between 1951 and 2001 we expect only 20 per cent growth, with some regional shifts but no major migrations.

But there is one demographic change which results from a slowdown in population growth: the change in age distribution. Our population is ageing and since most new household formation is among the under-35s, we can expect owner-occupation growth to slow. All this might point to a very flat picture for both owner-occupation and for the rented sector. Yet the housing problem is by no means solved. First, there are preferences for better housing, which can only be realised by policies which encourage refurbishment and renewal – arguably the pendulum has swung too far away from the excessive 'slum clearance' of the 1960s. There are still slums, and we are not clearing them. The house builders would also argue that increasing amenity and space demands can only be satisfied by a big relaxation of planning policies.

The Conservative Government set out planning policies that went in the opposite direction. John Gummer wanted 60 per cent of new homes in the next 20 years to be built on brownfield sites, rather than 50 per cent. Since the town and country planning association says there are not even enough sites to meet the current 50 per cent target, this is going to be a tough task – even ignoring the fact that many people do not presently want to live in urban areas.

We do need sensible planning policies, but these must distinguish carefully between sound environmental arguments and blatant nimbyism – however electorally powerful the nimbys may be.

More significantly, we are seeing a fragmentation of the traditional household. Social trends mean that households break up, and only partially reform, much more often than a generation ago, and surviving elderly parents live much longer, often alone.

All this means that average household size continues to fall. Some economists even argue that this is a natural force – that in a completely unrestrained market we would all live in one-person households! Be that as it may, we have seen average UK household size fall from 2.7 in the 1980s to 2.5 today and to a projected 2.3 by the year 2011, by which time it is expected that 35 per cent of all households will be single-person. So the demographics point to not much population growth, but still a significant growth in households as the average household size continues to shrink. How should we be looking to satisfy the needs of these households in the next 25 years – should they buy or should they rent?

Janet Ford has examined the future for owner-occupation in more detail, but this is the Halifax view.

Market research continues to underline a preference for home ownership. In research commissioned by CML in 1993, just after the worst years of the housing recession, over 80 per cent of adults saw owner-occupation as their ideal tenure. This figure was little changed from the late 1980s. Over 90 per cent of most adults actually expected to be owner-occupiers within ten years. More recent research in the 1994/95 'Survey of English Housing' also showed strong preference for owner-occupation with around 25 per cent of public sector tenants saying they intended to buy at some stage. Over 60 per cent of private tenants indicated a similar intention, however, the main reason why other tenants questioned said they did not intend to buy was simply lack of money. It is this factor, this realism, which makes one just a bit cautious about planning on the basis of figures indicating such high levels of owner-occupation. There will always be a gap between expectations and reality and even after the 1990s recession many people do not realise that there are much better and safer ways to invest money than in housing.

If this is not the case, and land scarcity forces house prices up more than earnings, hopes and expectations will be dashed as prices move away from prospective buyers. With most of the growth coming from one-person households, affordability is even more of a problem. Sustained low inflation rates – or even zero inflation with prices falling in some years – would affect people's attitude towards home ownership. If, in the first place, there is no inflation to protect against, and in the second place housing is not a very good protection anyway, the well-off middle class could well revert to leasing rather than buying, just as at the turn of the century. This could certainly apply to those whose jobs are mobile, nationally or internationally.

Another reason why we should not plan for owner-occupation rising to 80 per cent or more is that we face a changing labour market. Even if we were not, the very fact that the growth of home ownership continued to bring in more and more people on lower incomes whose jobs were inherently insecure would give pause for thought. But there are changes that go beyond this. Between 1981 and 2001, the UK economy will have lost 2.3 million full-time jobs and gained 2.7 million part-time jobs. By the turn of the century part-time employment will account for a quarter of all employment – and 52 per cent of all employees will be women. The usual reaction to these figures is to tell mortgage lenders to recognise realities, get their act together and produce more flexible mortgages. So we should, and so we are doing, but we can't disguise the fact that these changes in the jobs market alter the nature of risk and the processes of risk assessment.

Insurance is only a very partial answer and may well be unaffordable. We will be more cautious and so will potential borrowers. If there is one thing we have learned in 143 years of mortgage lending it is that we get no thanks for letting people take on commitments they come to regret! We could, of course, be wrong and the 80 per cent home ownership figure could be attained if we achieved continued and strong UK economic growth and high employment, leading to a big increase in personal wealth and real incomes. Not only would that improve affordability by reducing the 'house prices to earning' ratio, it could also produce a much stronger personal tax base and allow a strong welfare state to be sustained. However I do not think this will happen. I believe we can look to 2–3 per cent growth a year in what is a mature economy. The really big increases in national income will be restricted to those economies going through their own industrial revolutions.

We at the Halifax plan for a UK owner-occupied sector hovering just above the 70 per cent mark, compared with around 67 per cent today. Maybe 45 per cent will have mortgages, so we will still be dealing with a massive market of up to £500 billion. Natural turnover will generate a continued strong mortgage demand. With deregulation there will be continued intense competition – and this will mean some product and service differentiation. At the margins, borrowers will pay for the added value that comes from tailor-made products and personal service. But the huge middle market will be price-driven – a commodity market if you like – and the winners will be those with the lowest costs, the greatest efficiency and the best distribution systems.

Social renting

Can I now turn to the subsidised rented sector – social renting, if that term is politically correct. At the risk of grossly oversimplifying, the first problem here is that the supply is inadequate – certainly nowhere near the actual demand, let alone the potential demand. And the second problem is that this government and any government must be concerned about the huge costs of allowing supply to meet demand. Conservative governments cut back heavily on capital spending while sustaining revenue spend. We can see the same in health and education. It may, in part, be philosophical; a belief that additional capital spend will generate its own demand and that demand will have to be subsidised. Build a 600-bed hospital to replace a 300-bed unit and, sure enough, all 600 beds will be filled. Or it may simply be that in the annual battles which form part of the public spending round, capital is always easier to cut than revenue.

It certainly seemed that this was the case in the 1996 budget. The savage cuts in the Housing Corporation's capital expenditure programme were met with justifiable cries of outrage from the housing associations. Expecting private finance to close the gap is simply unrealistic. The result of these cuts must be to reduce the number of new social lettings in 1998 and beyond – to perhaps 45,000 a year. This is less than half of what most think is necessary. Capital spending on social rented housing now relies heavily on the private sector, while the revenue costs of subsidies – namely housing benefit – have gone through the roof, to an estimated £12 billion in 1996–97. In theory, this switch from capital to revenue should be efficient, because subsidies are income-related and as incomes rise the subsides fall. Capital grants are a sunk cost. In practice, of course, it isn't like this, and the ever-rising cost of housing benefit must be a major concern to this and any future government.

Since the 1988 Housing Act, £10 billion of private finance has been injected into social housing. It has funded the work of housing associations in two areas. First, in the mixed-funded, HAG- (housing association grant) supported development work. Second in financing the transfer of housing from local authorities to newly created housing associations through the programme of large-scale voluntary transfers. The Halifax is, in fact, currently funding over 100,000 housing association homes under these programmes. This work is making a very important contribution. But – to date – private finance has not been used in any volume to tackle the most serious areas of social deprivation and physical decay in our inner city areas. I think that there is much that private finance can achieve in these areas. But as ever, the key will be whether lending opportunities are structured so that they are fundable for organisations like ourselves.

Certainly the government seems anxious to press ahead with the Large Scale Voluntary Transfer Scheme (LSVTS), announcing new incentives in the budget. The aim is to double transfers from a planned 35,000 next year to 70,000 by 1998–99. There is a clear wish to transfer stock in outer urban areas, and indeed inner cities. But one of the big questions remains: 'can inner city stock be made fundable?' Earlier this year the government announced that over £100 million per annum would be made available to support 'estate renewal' challenge fund projects with another £70 million over three years announced in the budget. These are mainly inner city, local authority, areas where conditions are so difficult that the value of the property is actually negative. Government is therefore investing in repairing the stock with a view to transferring its ownership away from the local authority and bringing in private finance to fund the purchase price and ongoing improvements.

There are three key points arising from this programme. The first is that government is recognising that private finance on its own will not successfully fund renewal programmes in our most deprived inner city areas. As a concept then, the estates renewal challenge fund is very welcome. However, second, the planned rate of progress is very slow, with projected transfer programmes being limited to up to 50,000 dwellings per annum over the next three years. This equates to little more than 1 per cent of the housing stock currently in the ownership of local authorities. The programme needs to be expanded considerably if the problems of disrepair in public sector stock are to be addressed. But this of course brings us back to the issue of capital subsidy, which I have already mentioned. Third, our work with the initial 'estates renewal' challenge fund projects highlight the importance of appreciating that housing is but one part of the jigsaw, alongside a whole range of economic and social influences.

Improving the fabric of dwellings will achieve very little unless problems of economically inactive and socially deprived communities are tackled simultaneously. Without action on those fronts, it is difficult to envisage significant investment in bricks and mortar by lenders. It is very easy to become rather negative about prospects for the social rented sector. We should obviously try as a community to ensure that everyone has a decent home, but perhaps we should not think exclusively of quantity but also set ourselves targets in terms of quality. By this of course I mean the quality of service provided to the customer – that is, the present and future tenant.

I certainly think that it is a perfectly achievable objective for tenants to be valued as customers in just the same way as a Halifax investor is valued. I appreciate that the difference often is that the investor can take his or her investment elsewhere, whereas the social tenant, often caught in the infamous poverty trap, is not in such a position. Of course there are many examples of housing organisations adopting a customer service culture and we at the Halifax are as keen to contribute to these qualitative issues as well as the quantitative ones of the level of the supply of housing. We work with the Chartered Institute of Housing in areas of quality, for example, in sponsoring the production of the Institute's 'Good practice guide' for local housing companies, issued last year. We also work closely with the Housing Corporation and welcome their recent initiative to develop quality standards through defining what they have termed the social housing product.

Public rented housing has benefited substantially from private finance. But this success should not breed complacency. As with any lending, we must be sure not only about the underlying security but also about the borrower's covenant. And in the sector we are most active in – housing associations – the borrower's ability to sustain payments is heavily dependent on housing benefit. Rents must be at a level to sustain the association's income, service the debt and manage and maintain the stock. If they are not, and no more efficiency gains can be squeezed out of the association, then the only element that can give is maintenance, with the sort of disastrous consequences we have seen in some areas of local authority housing. The public spending implications are inevitable, as long as governments promise decent homes for every family. The only way to save money is to retract from such promises, but that would be another story.

Private renting

Can I now turn to private renting, and the role of institutions like the Halifax?

When we look at the rest of the industrialised world, the big difference between our housing markets and theirs is not the dominance of owner-occupation – four out of eleven OECD (Organisation for Economic Cooperation and Development) countries have a higher proportion than we do. It is the dominance of social renting over private renting – in Germany for example, the private rented sector accounts for 40–50 per cent of all households, three times the size of the social rented sector, while in France private renting accounts for around one-quarter of all households. Private renting is generally carried out by small-scale landlords. Large institutions are not a common feature in the rest of Europe. In this country the small landlord has been forced out – by legislation on security of tenure – and by rent control. New money could be better invested elsewhere, and existing money tied up in housing was released as soon as property became vacant, by selling into the owner-occupier sector.

Something interesting has happened since 1990. Private renting, having been in steady decline for a century, started to rise again – from 9 per cent to 10 per cent of the stock. Is this a marker for the future – a response to deregulation? Or is it simply a result of a bad owner-occupied market, where frustrated sellers took in temporary tenants? We do not know – but it may well be that the small private landlord could become 'respectable' again. Certainly finance will be available and many large lenders now offer loans specifically targeted at potential small landlords. In 1995 the government introduced the concept of the housing investment trust (HIT). This enables pension funds and insurance companies to invest in a fund which would provide private rented housing, thereby enabling the investor to be kept at arm's length from day-to-day management. The investor receives the same tax incentives for their investment in housing as they would for other forms of activity with investment trust status. The significance of HITs is rather more symbolic than practical at present. I say 'symbolic' because with the exception of the business expansion scheme, which was a short-term fiscal incentive in the early 1990s, this is the first incentive government has provided to the private rented sector for decades. By questioning its practicality, I am alluding to the fact that – at best – it will take some time for housing investment trusts to emerge. This is because a trust will have to be a minimum size of around £30 million in order to achieve a market listing. The one source of ready supply of rented housing that could enable such a critical mass to be established within a short time scale are the business enterprise schemes (BES). They will be coming available for purchase as original investors look to exit from the schemes over the next couple of years. Unfortunately the legislation governing HITs means that BES lettings, which are on an assured rather than shorthold tenancy basis, will not be capable of being purchased by a HIT. We are therefore left with the prospect of HITs as rather a more long-term prospect, if indeed adequate returns can be achieved for investors.

Many commentators are very negative about the prospects for corporate landlords in the private rented sector. It certainly is true that the vast majority of private landlords own one or two properties. I would like to see corporate landlords active in this sector because it is only in this way that the sector will grow in any substantial size. If we accept my earlier arguments about the rate of growth in owner-occupation, then a private sector providing good quality accommodation at market rents must be a welcome part of any thriving housing market. I do not share the doom and gloom of some commentators about the sector. I think we will see some corporate landlords emerge over the next few years, and I think that the BES properties will prove to be of interest to potential corporate landlords. But to achieve significant investment, I am quite sure that the problems surrounding housing investment trust type investment will have to be addressed by government. Only in this way will the potential returns to investors be adequate if we were to envisage a scenario of building good quality housing for long term renting at market rents. On a stand alone, non-incentivised basis, all our work at Halifax suggests that it is not possible to obtain in the short to medium term an adequate return on the investment.

Private Finance Initiative

Finally, some consideration must be given to the Private Finance Initiative (PFI), an initiative which is unlikely to bear much fruit before the year 2000. The PFI could be seen as a threat to private finance for social housing. There is not an unlimited pot of private finance, and government aims to attract £14 billion over four years. But there is a strong link. Good housing can only be sustained if the social fabric – health, education and transport – is of high quality. PFI initiatives can be considered for hospitals, NHS staff accommodation (maybe managed by housing associations), and local housing companies providing care in the community. Private finance could make a strong contribution to an integrated housing, health and social services framework. The first projects are coming to fruition and we are looking seriously at some of the first hospital redevelopment schemes.

Summary

To sum up, the Halifax sees a strong future for itself as a lender in the next century.

Obviously this means maintaining our support for residential mortgage business and introducing new products and services that will meet the needs of a changing market.

We do not expect to see the growth in this market that we experienced in the 70s and 80s; rather we expect to build on the experience we have gained in the social rented sector. If we can get the right sort of capital assistance from government, we can do more to help tackle social deprivation and housing decay in the big cities. Such government financial support is vital and lies at the heart of the social rented sector.

Finally, in the private rented sector we note with interest the apparent increase in small-scale private landlords, but we cannot yet be convinced that this is a genuine recovery. To reach German or French levels we would need a culture change that would take a generation or more. So we pin our hopes on the emergence of large, responsible, corporate landlords. Provided a future government is prepared to help with fiscal incentives that close the yield gap, we could see the big financial institutions being prepared to fund, and perhaps to become landlords in their own right. There is much to be done to sustain and improve the quantity and quality of our housing stock into the next century. You can be assured that Halifax, be it a building society or plc, will play its full part.

'What we Believe in'

This section details the basic values and beliefs on which St Anne's work is based.

The overall belief is that homeless people and people with special needs have the same rights as all other people and that they are entitled to be seen as and to play the full role of a member of society.

St Anne's Mission Statement summarises this belief by saying that we undertake 'to enable disadvantaged people to have the opportunity to secure and maintain the most suitable housing and to live as independent and full a life as possible'.

We see our role as to provide housing with care and support and to enable people to be regarded as full members of society. We recognise that prejudices exist in our society toward people who use our services and that this prejudice adversely affects them in a number of ways. We see it as part of St Anne's role to counter these prejudices in society generally. Many of our users perceive themselves as not being part of society. It is our role to enable them to overcome this perception.

Values and Beliefs

1. The need for a home is fundamental for most people and without this it is extremely difficult for any individual to build a satisfying way of life.

2. People with special needs and homeless people have the same rights as other people to satisfy all their human needs. They therefore are entitled to a good standard of:

   Physical care
   Housing
   Health care
   Social and sexual relations
   Education and training
   Jobs and positions of responsibility
   Spiritual fulfilment

We seek therefore to maximise aspects of individual's lives such as:

   Independence
   Autonomy
   Privacy
   Development of interests

We endorse the seven accomplishments identified by John O'Brien.

E Community presence: the sharing of ordinary places which define community life. Without focused effort, people with handicaps will be separated from everyday settings in segregated facilities.

E Choice: the experience of autonomy both in small everyday matters and in large life-defining matters, lifestyle, work, recreation and relationships.

E Competence: the opportunity to perform functional and meaningful activities with whatever level or type of assistance required.

E Status and respect: having a valued place among a network of people and valued roles in community life.

E Community participation: being part of a growing network of personal relationships which include close friends.

E Continuity: every individual should experience a natural progression in their lives. Where a change occurs in one area of life, care should be taken to minimise a disruption in others.

E Individuality: recognition of the uniqueness of each person ensuring that opportunity exists for individual self-expressions.

3.   To be able to meet these needs people are entitled to support, guidance and care.

4.   Consultation with users about important changes in their lives is important. The ideas and wishes of our users should not be dismissed simply because it may be difficult for them to convey or promote these ideas. However there may be limitations imposed on people's ability to make choices by illness, personal damage and the need to take medication. Judgements need to be made about the timing and method of consultations on the changes that affect residents or users bearing in mind individual abilities to cope with information and anxiety.

5.   All people should be regarded as having their own individual worth and therefore their own particular skills, insights, abilities and potential.

6.   Many people living in our accommodation are prescribed medication to control or alleviate symptoms of mental illness. Medication provides positive benefits but also negative side effects both physical, psychological and social. We see our role as encouraging users to cooperate with medical regimes but that we should work with users and others to ensure that medication is kept at a minimum possible level. We would normally encourage people to continue with medication, particularly if their past experience suggests that their health may deteriorate without this. However we will, if they so wish, actively support them in seeking to lower the level of medication as much as possible.

7.   The greater a person's ability to control their life then the greater is the expectation on them to accept the responsibilities of being a member of a household, family, group and society.

8.   St Anne's cannot provide all services to all its users. We believe that we must cooperate with other statutory, voluntary, private and other agencies in enabling users to achieve the highest possible quality of life.

'What We Do and How We do it': Aims and Objectives'

Aims

1.   To enable users to be seen as and to feel to be full members of society, not isolated minorities or individuals.

2.   To enable users to take as much responsibility for themselves as possible.

Objectives

1.   To provide a range of accommodation with the appropriate level of support for each user's individual needs.

2.   To design, implement and evaluate a programme of help and care which is based on the unique needs of each individual. This care plan will be operated in cooperation with colleagues within the organisation and in other agencies.

3.   To assess users on a continuous basis and hold regular reviews with users regarding their current situation and future plans.

4.   To provide a key worker for each user where this is appropriate. The key worker will aim to ensure that all necessary elements of the service are delivered to meet the users needs.

5.   To respect personal privacy.

6.   To support and encourage users in caring for themselves and the house in which they live.

7.   To offer social and emotional support to users as appropriate.

8.   To encourage and support users in making informed choices about their lives and to take responsibility for the consequences of their decisions.

9.   To encourage and actively support users where appropriate in their use of community resources.

10. To encourage users to develop friendships and to encourage participation in local facilities or groups.

11. We will encourage residents to express views and opinions and to organise themselves so as to formulate and express their views with regards to our service provision.

12. To act as an advocate for users where requested and where appropriate.

13. To offer continued support to former residents as appropriate and within the ability of available resources.

14. To observe the principles of confidentiality in all matters to do with users.

15. Eviction or barring from a service is always a last resort.

Staff

16. To develop a supported team approach to working.

17. To ensure clear channels of communication between staff and managers.

18. Staff will be provided with supervision and support where they are able to discuss their training needs and individual development.

Campaigning

19. St Anne's will in concert with other agencies campaign for the improvements of services for people with special needs through:

   a) Appropriate allocation of national and local resources.

   b) The reformulation of legislation and regulations where these adversely affect services.

   c) A more positive attitude by institutions and the general public towards people with special needs.

List of Contributors

Mike Blackburn joined Lloyds Bank in 1962, was appointed Chief Manager, Business Advisory Service in 1979 and in 1983 was seconded to be Chief Executive of The Joint Credit Card Company Limited (Access) and served on the boards of MasterCard International, EuroCard International and EFTPOS (UK). In 1987 he was recruited by Leeds Permanent Building Society to be its Chief Executive. In 1993 he joined Halifax Building Society as Chief Executive. Following the merger in August 1995 with Leeds Permanent Building Society, Halifax plc was floated on the London Stock Exchange on 2 June 1997.

Alan Butler trained originally as a psychiatric social worker at the University of Bradford. After practising for some years in both adult and child psychiatry, he joined the staff of Leeds Medical School.He spent four years investigating sheltered housing as a Rowntree research fellow and more recently was Pre-Clinical Dean within the Medical School. He is currently Chairman of the Division of Psychiatry and Behavioural Sciences. He is the author of four books and numerous papers on the themes of housing and mental health.

Alan Deacon is Professor of Social Policy at the University of Leeds. He is the author (with T. Dant) of *From Hostels to Homes? The Rehousing of Single Homeless People* (Avebury, 1989), and (with J. Vincent and R. Walker) of *Homeless Single Men: Roads to Resettlement?* (Avebury, 1995). He was editor of the *Journal of Social Policy* from 1986 to 1991 and has written extensively on social security and welfare reform.

Janet Ford is the Joseph Rowntree Professor of Housing Policy and Director of the Centre for Housing Policy at the University of York. She has written extensively about owner-occupation and was responsible for the first national survey of mortgage arrears and possessions in 1995. She has also undertaken research on the relationship between the housing market and the labour market.

Ian Law is Director of the RAPP ('Race' and Public Policy) Research Unit and Senior Lecturer in the Department of Sociology and Social Policy at the University of Leeds. His recent book *Racism, Ethnicity and Social Policy* (Prentice Hall/Harvester Wheatsheaf, 1996) draws upon his programme of research undertaken at RAPP since 1992. He is currently carrying out research on representations of 'race' in the British news media, ethnic managerialism in public services and racial violence in the UK. He is also convenor for the new centre for Ethnicity and Racism Studies established at Leeds in 1998.

Nigel Malin is Professor of Community Care and Divisional Research Co-ordinator at the University of Derby. He is editor of *Implementing Community Care* (Open University Press, 1994), *Services for People with Learning Disabilities* (Routledge, 1995) and *Reassessing Community Care* (Croom Helm, 1987). His main teaching has been social policy on health and social work programmes and he is currently undertaking research on clinical supervision and practice ethics in learning disabilities services and leading planning of a Community and Social Care Research Forum in Southern Derbyshire.

Fiona Spiers is Director of Development at Yorkshire Sculpture Park. After studying at the University of Edinburgh, she worked on the editorial team of *The Frederick Douglass Papers, The Black Abolitionist Papers* and *The William Wilberforce Papers*. She has published several articles on slavery and abolition and on African-American history. A career change led her to the voluntary sector where she was Appeals Manager at St Anne's Shelter & Housing Action before moving to her present position.

Gerald Wistow is Director of the Nuffield Institute for Health at the University of Leeds and Professor of Health and Social Care. He is the co-author and co-editor of 12 books and numerous other publications on the personal social services, the NHS and community care. His most recent books include *Social Care Markets* (Open University, 1996), *Options for Long-term Care* (HMSO, 1996) and *Psychiatric Nursing Revisited* (Whurr Publishers, 1998). He has been a specialist adviser to the House of Commons Health Committee since 1990 and is Deputy Chairman of the Leeds Community and Mental Health Services NHS Trust.

Subject Index

Author Index

CPI Antony Rowe
Chippenham, UK
2018-08-03 16:29